THIS DYNAMIC WORLD

Charles W. Morgan

authorHOUSE®

AuthorHouse™
1663 Liberty Drive
Bloomington, IN 47403
www.authorhouse.com
Phone: 1-800-839-8640

First published by AuthorHouse 6/11/2010

Printed in the United States of America
Bloomington, Indiana
This book is printed on acid-free paper.

ISBN: 978-1-4490-6717-5 (e)
ISBN: 978-1-4490-6716-8 (sc)

Library of Congress Control Number: 2009914322

DEDICATION
To Truth.

"Ye shall know the truth and the truth shall make you free."
St. John 8:32

CONTENTS

FIGURES

ACKNOWLEDGEMENT OF SOURCES

God is truth. If there be any truth in this book, it comes from God. If there be any non-truth, that comes from me and people like me who do not know the whole truth. It is my foremost desire to learn more of the truth of life, and to share it with others as best I can.

MY SOURCES:

The Bible and the Christian Way

The *Bible* is my first source of ideas and information. No two people interpret the *Bible* in exactly the same way. Each of us grows in our ability to interpret as our level of consciousness increases. So it is that I have to understand the Bible so that I can get from it the answers to the questions that will save my life and the life of this dynamic world. There is more, however. All of the apostles, prophets, teachers, and evangelists in the *Bible* have challenged us to get knowledge wherever we can find it and so I have found mentors and counselors that I trust and whose thinking I have proved.

Paramahansa Yogananda and the Hindu Way

My second source is the life and work of the Hindu Yogi (master or teacher – rabbi, sensei, doctor), Paramhansa (also Paramahansa) Yogananda. Born Mukunda Lal Ghosh in Bengal, India in 1893, he received a British Indian education and then sought the life of a Hindu master. His guru (inspirational mentor) was Sri Yukteswar, who gave him a new yogi name of Yogananda ("bliss through divine union with God"). He mastered the meditative discipline of Kriya Yoga, a very ancient Hindu teaching which includes considerable Buddhist thought. He gained the title of Paramhansa or "Supreme Swan" meaning "supremely illuminated one."

He was the first yogi to come to the west. After a cross country lecture tour, he settled in Los Angeles where he established his headquarters for an international *Self Realization Fellowship*. He had founded a school for boys in India and now he founded *ashrami* (spiritual retreat centers… something like a monastery) all over the United States. His disciples attended him in these temples of learning. He died in 1952. His teachings and a history of his efforts are collected in his *Autobiography of a Yogi* by Paramhansa Yogananda, Crystal Clarity Publishers, 1946. Republished by the Self Realization Fellowship, LA, CA 1983.

Harold Benjamin and Levels of Life

My third source is the late Dr. Harold Benjamin, Dean of the School of Education at the University of Maryland, 1946-47. He guided me through a master's degree in education and taught me the wisdom of looking at life in *levels* of growth.

Paul R. Mort and Areas of Life

My fourth source is Dr. Paul R. Mort, head of educational research at Columbia University in New York, 1950-51. It was there that I wrote my doctoral dissertation called "A Dynamic System of Evaluation." This became the basis of my book, *This Dynamic World*, which I wrote in 1959-60 and published locally in 1962. Dr. Mort taught me the need for looking at many *areas* of life to find the truth.

Ruth Montgomery and the Others

My fifth source is Ruth Montgomery who, in her many bestselling books, such as *Aliens Among Us* (Putnam, 1985), exposed me to the beliefs of the Christian psychics Jeanne Dixon and Edgar Cayce. I, as well as many followers in America, consider Edgar Cayce to be a prophet. Their way of analyzing the past to predict the future I found very motivating and very inspiring.

George King and the Astral Plane

My seventh source is the Englishman who emigrated to America and lived out his life in Los Angeles, Dr. George King, founder of the Aetherius Society, and his book *We are Responsible* which gives his theory that human mass negativity causes natural as well as social disasters. Negativity causes conflict which causes war, disease, revolution, "the lot" as the English say. He taught me that we are all free. We have independent agency. Because we are free, we are responsible for ourselves and for our world. When we look at bad things happening, we must conclude, King taught me, "We do it to ourselves." Child and grandchild of English country psychics, he also wrote *You Too Can Heal*. He teaches that people will be blessed and, indeed, healed, if they are prayed for.

After six years of selfless service as a volunteer firefighter and rescue worker in war ravaged London, the 26 year old King discovered Hindu and Buddhist yoga. He said he had a revelation. A voice told him, "Prepare yourself! You are to become the voice of interplanetary parliament." Shortly afterwards, he channeled his first message transmission purporting to come from an advanced spiritual being living on Venus and using the pseudonym "Aetherius."

From this came King's new religious movement, the "Aetherius Society." From King I learned about beings all over the universe that communicate telepathically and transport themselves by astral projection. King entered into many trances wherein he channeled these other beings in these other dimensions. He told the world about the dangers of too much technology that increased materialism and too little technology that took us toward spiritualism.

Aquarianism in a New Age and the Aquarian Gospel of Jesus Christ

My eighth source is the religious movement in late 19th and early 20th century America called Aquarianism which relies upon *The Aquarian Gospel of Jesus Christ* and which gave rise to *New Age* thought, worship, and culture.

According to *Wikipedia*, Levi H. Dowling, 1844-1911, was the son of a Christian minister during the religious revival in Midwest America before the Civil War. At age thirteen, the young man was debating local ministers on points of theology. He argued against eternal damnation, predestination and other decidedly "unchristian" sectarian doctrines. At age eighteen, in 1862, the young man began preaching in his father's church. But the Civil War raged and he served as a U.S. Army chaplain during the war. After the war, it seems he felt that Christianity as he had been taught it was too narrow. It inadequately explained how the universe really worked. He couldn't really minister to the needs of people with incomplete doctrine and fragmentary powers.

At the turn of the 20th century this Midwestern preacher and Civil War veteran was learning about a completely non-Christian religion from the other side of the world that met unmet needs for him and his following.

He recorded his revelations in what he called the *Akashic Record*.

Again, according to *Wikipedia*,

> The akashic records (akasha is a Sanskrit word meaning "sky", "space" or "aether"[ether]) is a term used in theosophy (and Anthroposophy) to describe a compendium of mystical knowledge encoded in a non-physical plane of existence. These records are described to contain all knowledge of human experience and the history of the cosmos. They are metaphorically described as a library and other analogues commonly found in discourse on the subject include a "universal computer" and the "Mind of God". Descriptions of the records assert that they are constantly updated and that they can be accessed through astral projection. The concept originated in the theosophical movements of the 19th century, and remains prevalent in New Age discourse.

They guided the world to what is now called New Age religion, spirituality, culture, and society. I may say they opened me to input from all of humanity as I tried to learn intellectually but also use my senses to find the possibilities of a human physical body.

This whole movement focused on the end of the world as we know it not in a cataclysmic way but in a benign joyous way as the passage from the (dark) Age of Pisces into the (light) Age of Aquarius. Hence the terms Age of Aquarius, Aquarianism, and New Age.

In 1908, Levi Dowling (self) published his reformulation of Christianity as *The Aquarian Gospel of Jesus Christ* (re-published in 1997 by Adventures Unlimited). He proclaimed that he was inspired to receive this gospel by revelation from ancient Aquarian Masters who, in life, had studied under the Prophet, Elihu, in a school of the prophets at Zoan in Egypt at about the time of birth of Christ. Thus it is suggested that perhaps Joseph visited Zoan when he took Mary and the child, Jesus, to Egypt to escape Herod.

The Aquarian Gospel taught me that there are, in a manner of speaking, many Christs and, indeed, there is a Christ within each of us That is to say Jesus of Nazareth, called the Christ, physically traveled and also sent his spirit to many more places and into many more people than we had supposed. Also, there are many more "sons of God" coming down to inhabit founders of spiritual movements and religions.

This explains spiritual leaders in all places and in all times who perform the function of Christ the savior and the enlightener under different names. These are the Hindu *avatars* (Sanskrit for "those who come down [from heaven to earth]") expanded out by Aquarianism to explain the seeming validity of Jesus, Buddha, Moses, Mohammed, Hindu saints, and so on.

The Aquarians put all of this into a formal religion and started a church, called the Christine Church, which fostered the beliefs and goals of the Aquarian Gospel of Jesus Christ. This church has evolved into the New Age religion we have today.

From this source I get a truly universal, enlightened vision of everything called forth by Jesus, the Hindu yogis (including the one I have relied on – Paramahansa Yogananda), the Buddha, Moses descending from the mountain, even Mohammed coming forth from his cave of refuge. I can see a crystalline new age of harmony, hope, love, and beauty for our struggling world.

Astronomy and astrology…What the Heavens Know

My ninth source is what I have learned of astronomy and astrology.

From very ancient times in all cultures there has been a reliance on study of the stars, planets, sun, and moon, their movement relative to each other and the effects of such movements upon our planet Earth. *Astronomy* is this study for the purpose of navigation, agriculture, and predicting (possibly even mitigating) collision between Earth and bodies from outside Earth.

Astrology is this study for the purpose of understanding human history and predicting the human future. Human behavior on Earth and the human effect on Planet Earth are, says astrology, the result of alignments and arrangements of constellations of stars, planets, the sun, and the moon. Astrology seeks to explain and predict global and, more particularly, human development, human conflict, climate change, climate shift, and pole shift, through the passage of ages, eras, or periods.

Every culture has an astronomical as well as an astrological system. Each astrological system has its own *zodiac* (Greek for "circle of animals") with a star chart mapping out these ages of astral cycles. The ancient Egyptians had theirs. The classical civilizations of pagan Greece and Rome had theirs. The Zoroastrian Persians had theirs. Jainist and Hindu India has its own system similar to the Persian. The Chinese had theirs (which were and are used over all of East Asia). The Semitic Arabs (pre and post Muslim) had theirs. Sub Saharan Africa has several. Polynesian island dwellers and seafarers had theirs. Meso America saw several systems, the best known and most relied upon of which is Mayan astrology (as well as their astronomy).

All of these astrological systems were integrated into their associated religions in the service of their cultures. They all explain God's will and the consequences of not doing God's will. That is, they all predict the future – both (or alternately) joyous and dire.

By these systems, I have learned that there is a lunar cycle, a solar cycle, and an astral cycle. All of these cycles take us through periods in our history. All astrology agrees that we are coming to the end of an age or period where there will be a conclusion to our way of life as we have known it and a beginning of a new perfected age.

Karl Jung and Analytical Psychology

My tenth source is the science and spirituality of Karl Jung. I actually became aware of Karl Jung and his analytic or Jungian psychology *after* I had formed my philosophical and spiritual beliefs. I am amazed and awed by how what I evolved in my mind comes out pretty much the same as the mind of Jung.

Science, Mathematics, and Philosophy – the Quantifiable Facts of Life

I have found counsel on how to apply the big ideas I have learned in my spiritual journeys to practical application in the "real" world of "physical" human life. In this book, I try to state what, exactly, I want people to do. This has, in turn, introduced me to very technical and practical philosophers, from east and west, from Aristotle to Confucius, with their theories, conclusions, and prescriptions for happy life and the temporal salvation of mankind.

From Plato to Aristotle to Einstein, from life to liberty to the pursuit of happiness, this is the Greek *episteme* or theory. With these sources I can respond to the great issues with what the data say we should do. Greeks call this *techne* or technique or technology. This is an assortment of systems that link steps we can take to apply theory to practical application. Doing it, getting the job done, is *practe* or practice, actual craftsmanship and skill. Here I use my own education from all my sources to make my judgment as to what we should do.

Thus it is that, while I have tried to be a good scholar and while I might be referred to as the legal author of *This Dynamic World*, in reality I channel many sources and contributors from every soul in existence in one way or another. "For I of myself can do nothing." (John 5:30)

PREFACE TO THE SECOND EDITION

I was discharged from the 75th Infantry Division on November 5, 1945. I walked out the gate of Camp Patrick Henry in Virginia and boarded a train that would take me home to Maryland. All the way home I felt tremendous joy just to be alive and I thanked God continually for saving my life. As I rode along, I thought about how all my experiences since leaving home had greatly expanded my consciousness and I was more and more impressed that I had some part to play in showing the world to the world. Pfc. Morgan, Charles W. was having a utopian vision. A statement of purpose and a prescription was forming in my mind. I knew I just had to write my book.

As I reentered civilian life, I got back into graduate school and began to learn beautiful concepts that I could use to describe the past, present, and future of the world. Also, the spiritualism that I was learning was showing me what I should be recommending to my readers as a plan of action for the preservation and salvation of the good in humanity and in the world.

I learned how to organize the history of planet Earth and of mankind into *eras*. Within each era, I could identify *levels* of development. I began to make recommendations as to what we should be doing in all of our *activities* to advance to the highest level in this, the final era.

By 1951, while I was studying at Columbia University in New York, my draft of my doctoral dissertation was becoming the book that I had seen. I had an opportunity to show the draft of my book to Eleanor Roosevelt when she was in New York as US ambassador to the United Nations.

The years passed and advanced technology simply exploded upon the scene. The book went through many revisions, as I observed onrushing change in an extremely dynamic world. Finally, I attempted a national publication of *This Dynamic World* in 1991.

In my preface to the first edition, I wrote, "This work shall be a drive to raise the consciousness level of all people and to begin to cleanse the world. Mankind needs to become creators and cleansers, not consumers and polluters."

I described this imperative progress as a *great transition* for the crossing of a *critical line* from the level of life that we have known to the highest and saving level.

Now it is 2009. I have had to react to even more sweeping change. So it is that I have come out with his *Second Edition* of *This Dynamic World*. We are truly at the end of one age and the beginning of another. My sources of practical knowledge and spiritual enlightenment all agree that hate, fear, Dark Age habits, Dark Age dogmas, and planetary destruction must all give way to an enlightened life. At the end of my life, I truly believe that this plan that we have created will make it possible for all individuals and groups to have common ground for identification and cooperation with one another.

This is a *crusade for worldwide biorelativity*. That means, we pray for each other; we worry about each other; and we help each other. We actually do work to raise the lifestyle and the thinking of every person on earth. We use our excellent plan to cleanse the earth and raise ourselves from the lower levels of past ages to the highest levels of happiness and success. I say "we" and "our" because, remember, my sources and I are all your representatives, spiritually receiving your ideas and righteous desires. "For I of myself can do nothing."

I most earnestly pray that you will become as excited and motivated by this new book that you hold in your hands as I have been ever since I first wrote it down 64 years ago.

Charles W. Morgan
Shrewsbury, Pennsylvania
August, 2009

INTRODUCTION

A DYNAMIC WORLD

The time has come for a spiritual cooperative (not communist collective), holistic, *planetary community* as the only practical way forward to a new age with a new dynamic.

In 1991 I wrote, "Advanced technology is swiftly reducing the functional size of the earth to a point where each of the 5.2 billion people live in (each other's backyards). In 2009, the population of our world is perhaps 6.2 billion. I say perhaps because population grows so fast that it is impossible to say the total number of people at any given moment.

In 1945, my buddies and I were carried across the Atlantic on an ocean liner in seven days. In 2009, today's soldiers and their buddies are carried home from Iraq and Afghanistan on the other side of the world in an airliner in 14 hours. That includes time on the ground in Europe. Your neighbor's rocket and its pollution can encircle the globe, *your globe*, in 90 minutes.

We live in a dynamic world. According to Webster's, the Greek word *dynamikos* means "energetic, forceful, continuous change; continuous activity; productive activity or change." This noun comes from the verb "*dynasthai...* to be able; able." I conclude that such change is driven by a systematic process.

The dynamic of our world is *relative contraction*. Of course, our planet is no bigger or smaller than it has ever been. It has as much water and earth and atmosphere as it has ever had because our environment is a closed system. However, the *availability* of land and water and oxygen in the air for the use of exploding numbers of people have all changed and will continue to change at an ever accelerating rate. Relative to our past, our living space and the resources we need to sustain life are all shrinking.

The result of this dynamic contraction is ever increasing *conflict* between have's and have not's both within and among nations. The Christian dynamic of" Love thy neighbor as thyself...share and share alike...faith, hope, and charity" is under greater stress and disrespect than even at the time of Christ himself.

PLANETARY COMMUNITY

Therefore, the time has come for a Christian cooperative (not communist collective), holistic, *planetary community* as the only practical way forward to a new age with a new dynamic. We create it in futurist science fiction; now we must create it in real life.

That is the main reason I wrote this book so long ago, a book I began to visualize the day in 1941 I was drafted into the armed forces to help fight World War II . If I were one of those lucky enough to live through it, I decided, I had to find out the real reason why we allow ourselves to become engulfed in anything as barbaric as war. Then, as terrible as was the conventional war in Europe, the atomic climax of the war in Asia was infinitely worse.

Since the first atomic bomb was dropped August 6, 1945, an all-out nuclear war was avoided mostly for one reason. *No one could win an all-out nuclear war.* There can be no victors in a nuclear war regardless of who strikes first, because the radiation fallout would encircle the globe and kill the killer, too. In the 1950's, the preoccupation of any futurist was nuclear war.

During the 50's, 60's, 70's, 80's, and 90's, there were 140 wars and rumors of war. All of them involved or threatened to involve the two sides in that "cold" war. There was always the threat of "escalation" to the nuclear brink.

During that time over 1700 nuclear warheads were tested. Therefore, from Hiroshima to the Nuclear Test Ban Treaty, the fact of the matter is we have been suffering at least some of the effects of nuclear war. Instead of creating a bit of heaven on earth we created a bit of hell on earth. We finally got control of the testing but a remnant of the threat is still with us.

The world now finds itself in the middle of another strange dilemma. There are not only no victors in the nuclear war, but there might be no winners in a nuclear peace. The traditional nuclear powers "build down" and break up their nuclear arsenals, but more and more countries attain nuclear weapons to defend against or intimidate ancient rivals.

We have moved on from the great confrontation of capitalism and communism (although that confrontation is making a comeback in the wake of the global economic crisis), but the world now confronts the next "big idea" in possibly nuclear armed, global war between ideologies disguised as religions.

Islamic and Christian fundamentalists relish the chance to re-enact the crusades with 21st century communications and weapons.

The doctrine of "Revolutionary War" and the "War of National Liberation" articulated by Trotsky, Mao, Ho, and Che is followed by stateless war using terror as a tactic. This is the new thing that works in global conflict, the new way to achieve the old goal of conquest and control. And all of this can now feature small, "dirty," nuclear weapons.

Also, we face a holocaust of another sort with the failure of economic globalism and its environmental impact. As with genocidal holocaust or nuclear holocaust, in this new situation, world governments face very nearly the same circumstances, have made the same mistakes, and committed the same crimes.

What a Tower of Babel! When will we ever awaken? If mankind is not soon brought to its senses the dire predictions of our great prophets just might happen. Super bomb or super storm, our destruction of our planetary environment is so great we could trigger massive earth changes strong enough to destroy all modern nations *as we know them*.

"As we know them…" How I do remember that phrase. It was in 1953 that I had the privilege to meet with Mrs. Franklin D. Roosevelt twice: once in Washington D.C. and once in New York City. We talked about the early draft of my book and its proposal for using immigration (or gathering) to cleanse and unify the world. I thought like Emma Lazarus who wrote in her dedicatory poem for the Statue of Liberty

Give me your tired, your poor, your huddled masses,
Yearning to breathe free.
The wretched refuse of your teeming shore.
Send these, the homeless, tempest tossed to me.
I lift my lamp beside the golden door.

I believed that a program of well organized *in-migration* to the United States would promote shared knowledge and build constructive attitudes that could prevent the war we all saw and dreaded. Now, in 2009, I note that one third of all college and university students in the United States are from other countries. Higher education is now one of America's best exports. That is very good. The best and the brightest come here and see what they can do to elevate their own culture with the best and brightest ideas from all over the world.

On the other hand, war, crime, poverty, and environmental destruction are driving whole populations out of their countries and into ours. This *mass migration* destroys the very haven that beckoned the distressed people in the first place.

I now believe that the key to the holistic planetary community is human *distribution* over the unused land of each nation and development of higher and better uses of space per person or persons per unit of space.

Mrs. Roosevelt closed our discussions with one precise statement. She said, "We would not want to change America in any way *that we now know her.*"

WORLDWIDE CRUSADE FOR BIORELATIVITY

If Mrs. Roosevelt only knew some of the changes that are being predicted for America in the 21st Century if we continue in our reckless ways, how would she change her statement? The so-called developed nations are filling up with immigrants who bring the conflict with them. Better, I now believe, to change from an emphasis on immigration to an emphasis on a *World Wide Crusade of Biorelativity.*

Edgar Cayce and George King both postulated a parallel universe on a different astral plane inhabited by astral people they called *Arcturians*. Both Cayce and King taught that the Arcturians visited us by a combination of transportation and communication called *astral projection*. Their mission was to help us and to get us to help each other. Ruth Montgomery decided that these visitors to help were *Aliens Among Us*, but she agreed that their desire was to help us spiritually and to get us to help each other. Many people around the world would call this phenomenon *angels*, guardian angels and heavenly messengers. From this idea came the exhortation that we should be each other's guardian angels. We should be our brothers' keeper. This is *biorelativity.*

I, with one "still, small voice," call for this World Wide Crusade of Biorelativity. It must be a mass movement (an anti-violence, pro-love crusade if you can imagine that) to help raise the level of the thinking of all people throughout the world. It is a crusade of "love thy neighbor as thyself." These crusaders will work, pray, meditate, think, and live in harmony with all people on earth. It gets tough when anti-violence and pro-love run up against pro-violence and anti-love, but Jesus, Buddha, Gandhi, and King (George and Martin Luther) never said it would be easy; they only said it would be right.

All of this brings us back around to a confrontation with the unrelenting fact that we have come to what Dena Dyer in her article for the Christian Broadcast Network calls "The Red Sea Place." There is no way around our troubles. We cannot stay where we are. Destruction is coming up behind us. The only way is through and that will take a miracle.

We need that holistic planetary community of spirit projecting prayers and preaching good ideas. We can call it the power of positive thinking. We can call it harmonizing the ether. Plato called it "the music of the spheres" and "the form of the good." All Christians call it "the Plan of Salvation" or "the Plan of Happiness" (In his *Ethics*, Aristotle said that "Happiness is the rational activity of the soul in conformity with the principles of virtue"). For myself, I gather all these tasks into the *Worldwide Crusade for Biorelativity*.

We can do the right thing…or not. We are free and we are responsible. If we continue to rape Mother Earth and murder our brothers and sisters then, logically, rationally, with scientific inevitability, there will be world ending events. All the religions of the world predict the circumstances that will end the world as we know it. They reveal the events that must line up for the end of the world to be initiated. However, they warn against calculating the exact time because they know that, if we have a date and time certain for the end of the world, we will cease to strive to reform the world and save it. For example, Jesus said, "Take ye heed, watch and pray: for ye know not when the time is." (Mark 13:33) If we prepare for the end of days by repenting of our sins, we show God a good world and a godly people who make the world worth a new beginning after the old ending.

If these good things are not done, then we may cause our own demise and fulfill the prophecies about the end of days. There may, indeed, be an accelerating pole shift with resultant changes in earth orbit and obvious catastrophic results. Global warming may cause gradual but total desertification in an evil synergy with de-oxygenation. Earth would be on track to become like Venus or Mars. We are not supposed to rely on Christ to renew the earth in its paradisiacal glory. He will, but we will be judged if we worked against him instead of for him.

GROWTH, PROGRESS, AND PERFECTION

This brings us through the Red Sea place that we may call the Cleansing Age with its World Wide Crusade for Biorelativity. We crusade for common ground on which to identify and cooperate with one another. This is a not a crusade to kill, but a crusade to save.

Global spirituality can raise the lifestyle and the thinking of every person on earth.

There is a system in operation here which we can use to achieve our personal and global goals. Come with me now as I tell you the story of how I learned that system.

CHAPTER ONE
WHO AM I THAT I SHOULD PROCLAIM THESE THINGS?

THE EVOLUTION OF CHARLIE MORGAN

Older Charlie Morgan

I am Charles W. Morgan and I am 92 years old. You might call me a hillbilly schoolteacher with big ideas. I began as a Lutheran Christian. Teaching was my joy but farming was how I provided for my beautiful family. The big events of my century plucked me out of the highlands of western Maryland and started 68 years of exposure to the whirling currents of this dynamic world. Human, humble, not mystical, not metaphysical experiences taught me to find happiness in the immaterial and the spiritual.

I am an odd sort to be proclaiming a plan for global salvation. I've lived most of my life in rural, western Maryland. I came off the farm to go to college. All my years as a schoolteacher, I still owned and operated a farm. For decades, my neighbors called me a "hillbilly schoolteacher." Recently, a man with whom I was discussing my book blurted out that I was a "Hindu preacher!" I guess he meant that I was explaining a doctrine very strange to my country and yet doing it in the familiar manner of a Christian fundamentalist preacher. Why can't a hillbilly schoolteacher that leaves his farm every day to go to work (except for when he goes off to war on another continent) assemble the best spiritual doctrines from around the world to come up with a plan for the salvation of our world? Jesus was a carpenter. Moses was a shepherd. Mohammed was a merchant. Paramahansa Yogananda was a college student. George King was a taxi driver. Confucius was a government consultant. Siddhartha, who became the Buddha, was a spoiled prince in a minor Indian kingdom.

LUTHERAN FARMBOY

I grew up believing that there is an omnipotent, omniscient, and omnipresent God. I still believe that. I believe that God loves us and loves his universal creation. God is good. "And God saw everything that he had made, and, behold, it was very good." (Genesis 1:31)

Classic Farm Scene

I was born in Wolfsville, Frederick County, Maryland, in 1918. I was raised on a farm nearby. Many of the people around there were German settlers from the early 1700's. They were Lutherans. My family, the Morgans, was mostly English. Morgan, of course, is Welsh. We had Germans in our line and I married a German. At any rate, I was raised Lutheran. I went to church every Sunday in a beautiful little Lutheran church with its spire reaching up above Wolfsville and visible from the country around town.

Lutheran Church

In church, I was taught Lutheran Catechism. I learned the *Nicene Creed*. I learned that God was omnipotent, omnipresent, and omniscient. I learned that God was one and yet three. There was God the father, who in some mysterious and miraculous way was born of a mortal woman as God the son, and there was God the Holy Ghost, who was the spirit of God that inspired and protected us, if we were of his holy elect.

I learned the doctrine of *justification*. Our minister said that we are saved from our sins by God's grace alone, through faith alone, because of Christ's merit alone. He told us that God made the world and people perfect, holy, and sinless. However, our first parents, Adam and Eve, chose to disobey God. They trusted themselves more than they trusted God. Because of this original sin, we would all go to hell, if it hadn't been for the graceful sacrifice of Jesus Christ on our behalf. If we have faith in Christ, we will be saved from eternal damnation and get an opportunity to go to heaven. We have to demonstrate our faith by being baptized, and by taking the communion of the Lord's supper.

If we do all these things, then our "old Man of sin" is dead and we are reborn into a spiritual and eternal life. We can only do all these things if we come to a knowledge of our sinful life and repent and receive forgiveness.

In addition to the Nicene Creed, I was also taught the *Apostle's Creed*, which says that if we repent of our sins, throw ourselves on the mercy of Christ, submit to baptism, and receive all the sacraments, then, finally, through his grace, we are predestined to be saved in heaven.

The minister at his pulpit on Sunday and at the head of our class in catechism on a weekday were impressive influences on a disciplined little farm boy. I noticed, however, that these doctrines in these religious acts focused on what I was supposed to do to be good. They didn't tell me what I was supposed to do to help other people to be good. They didn't tell me what I was supposed to feel in order to master my fears and deal with bad things around me. And there were bad things around me that made me afraid.

One of my first dramatic experiences occurred at the age of five, It was summer, 1923, wheat harvest time, and my father was sweating behind three horses on a binder when he told me to go to the house and get him a pack of chewing tobacco. Naturally, I obeyed, but on the return trip, at the bottom of a hill by our springhouse, curiosity got the better of me. What does it taste like, I wondered? So I wiggled a tiny sliver out of a folded corner of the pack and stuck it in my mouth. WOW! Into the springhouse I flew to wash out the sting from my tongue. How can my father stand to put a whole chunk of that poison into his cheek for hours? No wonder it keeps him awake and on the job. His mouth must be made of leather.

That was both the beginning and the end of any thought of nicotine addiction. I had nothing to do with tobacco, except for passive breathing of the smoke coming from people committing cigarette-suicide around me. After getting that one bitter taste, I can understand about the deaths, but the scope of the 500 billion cigarettes per year addiction consumption leaves me in awe. My father's habit lasted until he was 40 and on his death bed. Rather than die, he stopped using tobacco and lived until age 89. But until he reached 40 his habit kept our family in poverty. We were often hungry and ill-clothed so he could buy tobacco.

My second horrendous experience came in the 1930's when the American people voted to repeal the 18th Amendment to the Constitution, called Prohibition. My father's addiction to alcohol was also of a suicidal nature. For the family it was murderous. Many were the times we nearly got killed by guns and cars. Nearly every spring about planting time, my father would go on a two-week drunk and leave home. Then my mother and we kids would try to find him in the neighborhood.

The repeal of Prohibition came as a shock to me as we struggled to survive in the poverty thirties. Why? I asked. Even today I ask why do we make it legal to have some 20,000 American citizens murdered each year in motor vehicles so that our "Christian" nation can "enjoy" alcohol at weddings, banquets, parties, celebrations, and all kinds of social and political events. Somehow, I feel I am asleep to reality, when they tell me that drugs are the largest cash crop in America, and the largest business. That is America?

Roman Ruins: Forum

My third awakening came in the 6th grade, when I studied Greek and Roman history. Truly, I admired the Greeks and the Romans in so many ways. It is even said that the great "Roman Peace" made it possible for Christianity to spread so far so fast. The one thing I could not understand was the fall of this great Roman Empire in 476 A.D. Why? Why would anything so great, strong and wonderful fall flat on its face? Why?

The answer seems to center around the word *cycle*. Even as a boy reading books, I could see that life has cycles or waves. A person or a nation works hard and tries to do right. This brings success and happiness. Then the person or community of people becomes proud and self satisfied. They enjoy power and wealth. Then the person or community becomes lazy and corrupt. Then they fail and fall.

Later I would listen to the elaborate explanations of historians and religious teachers who explained about creation and consumption, pleasure seeking and pain avoidance. I listened to metaphysical masters who had an explanation from the stars.

They insisted that our sun is a binary sun. Every 25,000 years it makes one oval orbit opposite its binary twin around an electromagnetic center. At the two points in the orbit closest to the electromagnetic center, earth people experience an age of great enlightenment, but some 6,250 years later, at either of the most distant points of the orbit, there is a dark age on earth.

The Dark Age was almost at its peak about 476 A.D., and the Romans became gross, sensual, and immoral. Responsible citizenship deteriorated and decayed. Barbarians from the north conquered Rome. Blame it on the sun? That is the way it sounds, but maybe that is an attempt to explain the cyclic war of good against evil – now good winning, now evil winning, with spirituality versus materialism. As I continued to grow up, I looked around and wondered if the Dark Age still lingered on in America today.

In my life as a teacher and as a parent, I have learned that kids ask why. It is not enough to just catechize. I later learned how to do something that my Lutheran minister never attempted. I learned how to ask and answer the question, "Why?"

INQUISITIVE COLLEGE STUDENT

In 1936, I left my home town of Wolfsville, dominated by the steeple of our little Lutheran church where I had received communion, to go to Frostburg College in Frostburg, Maryland. I studied education because I wanted to be a teacher. I wanted to help people live an advanced, not a primitive life. I went to college with the blessing of my family and our Lutheran minister. At Frostburg, I got a conventional and very practical liberal arts education.

But it wasn't enough. I wasn't getting what I needed to understand life and how to live. Then, as so often happens in the young life of a thirsty mind, a source dropped in front of me that changed everything.

A friend of mine at Frostburg told me about a Hindu yogi (whatever that was), named Yogananda. He had the title of "Paramahansa." This Yogananda had brought his Hindu way to America in 1920. Later, I would learn about Paramahansa Yogananda and become a student of this yogi, learning his yoga (his discipline). These new ideas fascinated a college student and I had to know more.

 If you knew what to look for in the media of 1930s America, Paramahansa Yogananda was in the news. He left India in 1920 to come to America because he wanted to share with western people the knowledge and power he had attained through what he called the "spiritual realism" and, indeed, science of the Kriya Yoga. His master, Sri Yukteswar, told him that, if he was going to do it, "It was now or never." Master Sri told Disciple Yogananda, "America is very efficient materially, but she needs the spirituality of India." There he was, in a group photo as India's delegate to the World Congress of Religious Liberals in Boston, 1925. There were the programs for his American lecture tour. There he was establishing his ashram – his retreat and school -- in Los Angeles for his Self Realization Fellowship. There he was visiting India and meeting with Mohandas Gandhi, the Mahatma. I was drawn to all this. It was warm and stimulating and comforting in a way that Martin Luther never was.

I graduated in 1940 and got the job I wanted, teaching elementary school to farm kids just like me. At the same time, though he was in his "ashram" in Los Angeles, California and I was up in the hills of western Maryland, I was sitting at the feet of a "Paramahansa," a Hindu yoga master and he was my guru.

All through my college days and my first teaching job and through four years in the Army, I expanded my consciousness with knowledge of Kriya Yoga as learned and taught by Paramahansa Yogananda. The war took Americans to India, and Mahatma Gandhi was in the news. I gathered more materials about reincarnation, seven chakras, Nirvana, Hindu saints living on cosmic energy, and the ultimate spiritual level of life. I was so excited that I made the mistake of telling my family back home about what I was learning. I sent them some of the pamphlets and tracts that I had found. They burned it all, because they thought it had something to do with evolution, which it does actually.

CHARLIE'S GONE FOR A SOLDIER

My fourth horrendous experience came in war. As a child, I saw my father talk to veterans who came to our farm. They talked about World War I, but it was not until my war that I got the real picture.

I was drafted in January, 1941. I was three years in the Air Force and the last year in the infantry. I spent six months in Europe. I got there after The Bulge and the 7th Army's invasion of Germany. I participated in the first months of the occupation of Germany. When I entered the 106th Infantry Division, they were pulled back off the front lines after the Battle of the Bulge, guarding 900,000 prisoners in a bombed out factory complex.

Young Charlie Morgan

May 8, 1945 was V-E Day and I got orders transporting me back to the States but NOT for discharge. I was assigned to the 75th Infantry Division, headed for the invasion of Japan. In the Mid-Atlantic, our 18,000 men aboard the Queen Mary learned of the first atomic bomb dropped August 6, 1945. The second one fell on August 9, 1945. V-J Day came on August 14, 1945. I could have been "passed through the fire to Moloch" (Leviticus 18:10) in Asia, except for the Japanese men, women and children who preceded me through the fire that August, 1945. I am a witness to the horrible devastation and degradation of human society resulting from war. I saw what people are capable of doing to people. I caught a glimpse of antichrist. Perhaps the most evil thing on earth today, nuclear war, saved my life.

They died that you and I might live. The least we can do is our best to see that the war-and-violence addiction of mankind stops. This is what I took away from my war experience. This will not be easy. Man has fought some 5,000 wars in the last 3,000 years and some 140 wars since World War II. Undoubtedly, war is another Dark Age addiction.

On November 5, 1945, I was discharged from the 75th Infantry Division at Camp Patrick Henry, Virginia. When I went out that gate and boarded a train for my home in Maryland, I was so glad just to be alive that I thanked God for saving me. Like so many others who come through such a trial of life and death, I realized I had to promise him that I would do what I could to make sure that nothing like this happened again. And so I promised him I would dedicate the rest of my life to searching for solutions to all of man's age-old problems that I had seen. I was 26 years old.

THE YOGI AND ME

When I got home, our minister came to visit me. He wanted to counsel me about what I was getting into.

I asked him, "Do you believe in reincarnation?"

He said, "No." That was the end of the counseling session.

PY Bio Book Cover

In 1946, Paramahansa Yogananda published his *Autobiography of a Yogi* and I drank in every word. The book had a momentous influence on a wide readership across western civilization. It was the first stirring of the turn to eastern spirituality by disaffected western youth and of the blending of eastern and western religions that would flower in the loud sixties following the silent fifties.

From Yogananda I learned that focus on material things is unworthy. Progress for a human being is passing through material considerations and focusing on the spiritual state. In both the Buddhist and Hindu way, this is *enlightenment* or *Nirvana*. If we can master this ability to progress, we find ourselves rising through levels of attainment. He described how he had passed through seven states of personal evolution, called *chakras*. Each chakra dealt with the functions of its level of life starting from the lowest, most basic level and rising to the highest, most refined level.

In moving through the chakras of personal development or evolution, we find ourselves moving through different levels in everything from food to building to occupations to relationships. For example, we move from eating animals to eating plants to eating sun or cosmic energy. In another example, we move from digestion and elimination to sexual function to solar plexus and breathing and on to heart and emotions and still farther on to voice and vision and imagination.

Kriya in Sanskrit means "action" or "deed." *Yoga* means discipline or doctrine. Therefore, perhaps Kriya Yoga can be said to be a set of actions or a doctrine of disciplined activities. At any rate, Kriya Yoga is a school for teaching what actions will bring about progress through all the levels of life to the highest, most spiritual, and most beneficial way of life.

Yogananda taught that we sit in a sea of cosmic energy. If we can learn the right yoga, we will feel that energy and draw it into us with our breath as though our brain were the mouth of God. That energy will then animate us and motivate us through the seven chakras. Yogananda taught all this in California. It is easy to see how his yoga became health-food, purification, putting out a good energy, good vibrations, and the whole California New Age terminology.

Yogananda explains these points with stories of Hindu and other saints. The one that affected me the most was the story of Giri Bala.

In the Hindu tradition of India, there is, as in the Christian and Muslim worlds, the idea of a saint – a person who has achieved a holy, inspired state of being in order to do good.

There is a story of a Hindu saint, born in 1868, named Giri Bala. She lived in an isolated Bengal village. Giri insisted that she had been a fat, gluttonous little girl with a neurotic attitude about food, self image, and acceptance (Is any of this sounding familiar?). She prayed for help to overcome her behavior and achieve a happy life. One day, a spirit guru (kind of an angel) visited her and taught her a spiritual technique called Kriya Yoga (The yoga taught to Paramahansa Yogananda). Once she mastered Kriya Yoga she was free from the need for earthly food and insisted that for the rest of her life (56 years) she did not eat or drink but lived on "cosmic energy."

When her story spread around her district, the ruler of that Indian state brought her to his palace to observe her. He released her after certifying that, indeed, she did not eat or drink anything and yet was in perfect health. Yogananda visited her and heard her story in 1924. Later, in his U.S. lecture tour, in his ashrami, and in his book, Yogananda touted the story of Giri Bala and other saints as showing how human beings could rise to the highest spiritual level and be sustained by cosmic energy from God. (pictured left together, 1936)

PY with Giri Bala 1936

THE SEVEN CHAKRAS

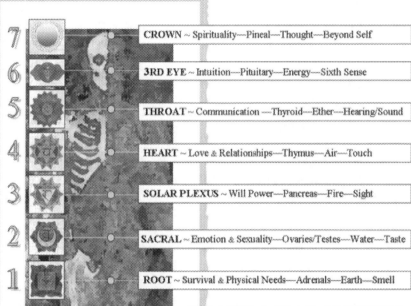

7		CROWN ~ Spirituality—Pineal—Thought—Beyond Self
6		3RD EYE ~ Intuition—Pituitary—Energy—Sixth Sense
5		THROAT ~ Communication —Thyroid—Ether—Hearing/Sound
4		HEART ~ Love & Relationships—Thymus—Air—Touch
3		SOLAR PLEXUS ~ Will Power—Pancreas—Fire—Sight
2		SACRAL ~ Emotion & Sexuality—Ovaries/Testes—Water—Taste
1		ROOT ~ Survival & Physical Needs—Adrenals—Earth—Smell

CHAKRA BALANCING

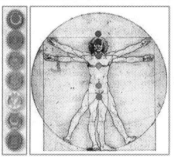

Giri Bala ~ 1936

Our **CHAKRAS** are like a set of gears that will run smoothly as a system when kept in balance with one another through such discipline as meditation, physical exercise, affirmations & prayer.

The famous **Giri Bala** achieved such a high level of this balance she no longer needed any nutrient other than cosmic energy to live.

FIGURE 1

There are Christian saints, Muslim saints, and Jewish spiritual communities like the Essenes as well as Lord Siddhartha who became the Buddha (the Enlightened One) all of whom embraced an *ascetic* way of life. This focuses on spiritual rather than material life and is not fixed on food, sex, or other material gratification. Indeed, Jesus fasted for forty days and forty nights to prepare for his ministry.

Fixation on sexual pleasure without love has been the downfall of great societies of our world. What I get from the Kriya Yoga, the Gospel of Jesus Christ, the teachings of the Buddha, Confucian Ethics, and the synthesis of all these doctrines in New Age Aquarian thought is that sex is for a purpose. That purpose is love in marriage that results in children. I have learned that the sex fluid is precious and the sex organs are the easiest to harm. Throughout history a symptom of social decay has been when sex kills instead of giving life. As we can become addicted to tobacco or alcohol, so we can become addicted to a degrading fascination with sexual pleasure. Along with alcohol, drug, or tobacco suicide, we can commit sex suicide. I say love God, not sex and your sex life will be glorious. Think of your beloved as a human being, not a sex object. Look on human beings as your spirit brothers and sisters whom you would never harm.

These doctrines of denial are actually liberation from slavery. For example, free yourself from the highs and crashes of processed food. Eat raw vegetables as much as possible. Cook vegetables as little as possible. Their enzymes help make energy in you from the action of the sun upon the chlorophyll in the plants (photosynthesis). The Hindus call this cosmic energy. Don't commit processed food suicide!

This belief that spirit and matter are extensions of each other or rather different manifestations of the same thing is behind the Hindu doctrine of reincarnation and the Christian doctrine of the Plan of Salvation.

The essence of both is that you do not die. You just give up your mortal body for a time until you advance to the next level of being. The story of Jesus and Lazarus shows us that the dead are alive. The truth is that we are all spirit children of God who grow up through life and death and life. I say believe you are a child of God. If you don't believe it, you won't act like it. The way you lived your previous life indicates how you live today. How you live today indicates how you will live in the next life.

George King said we do it to ourselves. What we do to the environment of life is what we do to each other and to ourselves. Raise the environment with love. Speak words of love. Lower the environment with hate, speak words of hate to bring about war, jealousy, and destruction. These are the real environmental disasters.

This, then, is a difference between deprivation and leaving behind physical desires. It may well be that living in the world but not being of the world is the correct way to live. The story of Giri Bala living without eating or drinking for 56 years inspires us to want better things. Giri Bala achieved the highest level of consciousness and connection. She left behind materialism and embraced spirituality. Her angel taught her to convert energy to mass by drinking in the benefits of the sun, the highest source of energy. Giri Bala learned to live on *cosmic energy*.

Yogananda never did without food and drink and he never expected anyone else to do that. He did, however, live a life of peace, love, and health. His yoga included an Indian *Ayurvedic health code* that kept him seemingly ageless. Yogananda decided when it was time for him to die. In 1952, he gave a presentation at the Biltmore Hotel in Los Angeles before which he mentioned to his guests that he felt like his time had come. He had been perfectly healthy up to that time, but after his speech, he slipped to the floor and was pronounced dead of heart failure.

The Forest Lawn Mortuary Director wrote this in a notarized letter:

The absence of any visual signs of decay in the dead body of Paramahansa Yogananda offers the most extraordinary case in our experience.... No physical disintegration was visible in his body even twenty days after death.... No indication of mold was visible on his skin, and no visible drying up took place in the bodily tissues. This state of perfect preservation of a body is, so far as we know from mortuary annals, an unparalleled one.... No odor of decay emanated from his body at any time....

I have meditated often on the concept that *the human body is a temple*. In 1 Corinthians 3:16, Paul exhorts the members of the Church of Jesus Christ, "Know **ye** not that **ye are** the **temple** of God, and that the Spirit of God dwelleth in you?"

Remember that I come from way back in the hills, up by the Alleghany Trail. One of our favorite dishes when I was little was fat back pork cooked with hominy or cornpone. Now, 80 years later, I eat a healthy diet and not too much of anything. I learned that moving through the chakras is the journey of a life time and that your soul cannot be perfected in only one life time. Giri Bala and Paramahansa Yogananda would say that the principle is to avoid physical and spiritual suicide by shedding bad inputs and searching for good inputs.

Start by eliminating addictions like drugs, cigarettes, and alcohol. Continue with bad meat, like pork. Continue on until you eliminate all meat. Continue with this process until you have eliminated *dependence* on material things. The point is to rise above your addictions and appetites to a spiritual life.

The idea of progressing through levels of personal development and the technique for progressing through levels of personal development lead inevitably to the basic Hindu doctrine of reincarnation. As each human individual has seven chakras, so the soul of each human individual passes through seven incarnations. That is seven births into seven mortal lives. God passes each soul through these lives so that in each life the soul will do better and gain more merit. Finally, a good soul will have perfected itself and pass out of mortality into a perfect union with God in a perfectly enlightened state called Nirvana.

You want to be a good soul and not a bad soul, because, if your soul is evil enough, you can be disincarnated. That is, God will prevent you from moving forward through your seven bodies, because you are wasting bodies and corrupting mortal human beings.

Thus it is that the Kriya Yoga of Paramahansa Yogananda as taught in America showed how to be good and why to be good. The Kriya Yoga of Yogananda insists that this is all scientific. Yogananda calls it *spiritual realism*.

Later in 1946, after I had studied *The Autobiography of a Yogi*, I learned that Hindu yogis revered and followed the principles of Jesus. I learned the concept of *avatars*. An avatar (in Hindi: "someone who comes down from heaven") is a manifestation of God and could be called a son of

God coming down to earth as a human being in order to lead the people back to God by his perfect example of how to live (and, in the case of Jesus, how to die).

Yogananda and others referred to *The Lost Years of Jesus* by Nicholas Notovich, published in 1894, which tells the story of how Notovich found Tibetan manuscripts in the Nepalese monastery of Himis that tell the story of the mysterious "Saint Issa." From these sources, Hindus came to believe that, in the lost years of Jesus, from age twelve to age 30, Jesus visited India. The Hindus also believe that there have been many manifestations of Jesus appearing and disappearing all over the world. Indeed, they believe that Jesus mastered the yoga of such complete control over the physical body that, like Hindu saints and yoga masters, he could dematerialize (disappear) and re-materialize (appear) at will. In other words, he could teleport. Actually, the *Bible* is full of stories of angels appearing and disappearing, is it not?

THE CONCEPT OF AVATARS

JESUS   BUDDHA   MOSES   MUHAMMAD   CONFUCIOUS

AVATAR, in Hindi: *"Someone who comes down from Heaven"*

in order to lead the people back to God by his perfect example...

FIGURE 2

I began to study the *New Thought* about Christianity and its bond with other ways to spirituality.

THE STARS SAY JESUS IS COMING

As the year 1946 came to a close, my head was buzzing and my heart was pounding with the inspiration and the motivation of Paramahansa Yogananda. I wanted to perfect myself by progressing through the seven chakras. I could see how the Kriya Yoga of self perfection could be applied to guiding the world through progressive levels of development. The individual can go through seven chakras seven times in seven lives, ending up in a state of enlightened perfection. The world, with all of humankind, has similarly been advancing through eras and climbing up through levels of evolution aiming at the same goal.

But I missed the Jesus of my youth. It was all right that Yogananda and the other gurus allowed Jesus a place in their system. Jesus was another one of their yogis. But I missed "Christ the Lord is Risen Today" and "Come Ye Disconsolate" and "A Mighty Fortress Is Our God." I didn't miss Martin Luther, but I did miss Jesus the Christ.

Levi Dowling

I realized I had to study more about my original Christian faith in order to compare it to this completely other way that I found so exciting and so hopeful. I was intrigued by the emerging *New Age* beliefs involving the *Age of Aquarius*. These *Aquarians* had created their own amalgam of all that was good in eastern and western religions.

I found out about another restless soul – Levi Dowling, the boy preacher of Ohio, who gave comfort to the boys in blue fighting for the Union as an army chaplain (preached a funeral sermon for Abraham Lincoln to Illinois troops) and then went on to fill his spiritual deficits with the calculations and predictions of astrology.

Levi Dowling was a powerful minister of Jesus Christ and then became a medical doctor and taught in the medical school of his alma mater, Northwestern Christian University in Indianapolis. He was determined to understand the physical basis of non-verbal, spiritual communication, which he called *etheric communication*. It made him a pioneer of electricity in medicine with such things as measuring brain waves. He perfected his ability to meditate until, he said, he was receiving communication from spirits and beings from other worlds.

He combined knowledge of the stars in their astral cycles, the spiritual science of Hinduism, the vision of Buddhism, and the practices of Taoism with his understanding of the gospel of Jesus Christ.

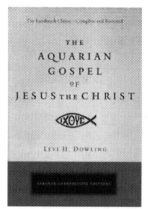

Aquarian Gospel

Levi Dowling proclaimed that this *Aquarian Gospel of Jesus Christ* was given to him as a revelation of the *Akashic Record* by the ancient *Aquarian Masters*. From these sources, he translated *the Aquarian Gospel of Jesus Christ* as an actual scripture. The essence of his statement and of the *Christine Church* that came from it is that Christ had many incarnations and was able to teleport himself to many places in his original incarnation and thus be the connection between all of the world's great religious systems.

Dowling taught that Jesus came in the dark and negative *Age of Pisces*. His mission as the Christ was to prepare us for the advent of the light and positive *Age of Aquarius*. Astrology foretold the birth of Christ by lining up planets to make a superstar. This "star in the east" guided three Zoroastrian astrologers to his birthplace.

STAR IN THE EAST

The three star belt of the constellation, Orion, are also known as the *Three Kings*. The three pyramids at Giza in Egypt are patterned after these famous three stars.

The pyramids are aligned to match the three stars with amazing precision.

On December 24th the *Three Kings* line up with and point to or "follow" the brightest star to appear that time of year, which appears low in the sky and is called *Sirius*, "the star in the East".

FIGURE 3

AGE OF AQUARIUS

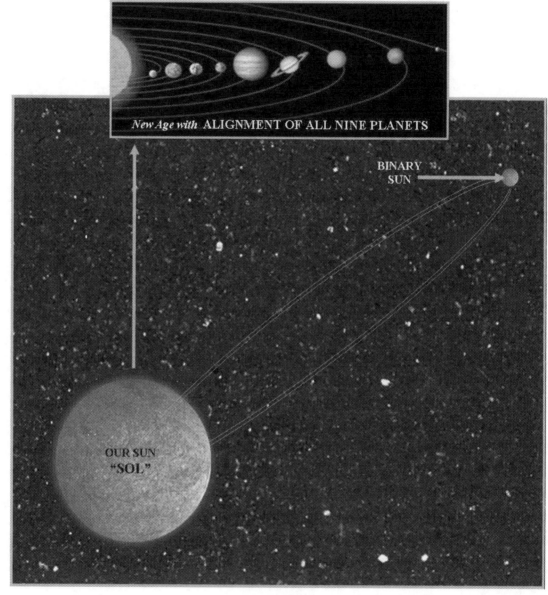

New Age with ALIGNMENT OF ALL NINE PLANETS

BINARY SUN

OUR SUN "SOL"

FIGURE 4

I enter my career in this dynamic world

In 1948, I carried all this into my new married life and my continuing education. I made use of the G.I. Bill of Rights to make a life for me and my new family. I got a Master of Education degree from the University of Maryland. I started a doctoral program at Columbia University in New York.

In my graduate program at the University of Maryland, my graduate advisor, good friend, and teacher of teachers was Dr. Harold Benjamin. His great academic contribution was a theory of human development through *levels*. His approach seemed to be an offspring of *Maslow's Hierarchy of Needs* with the most basic and physical of human needs at the lowest level and continuing upward through more emotional, then relational, then intellectual, and finally spiritual needs. Considering what I had been studying, it was eerily parallel to the human working upward through seven chakras and seven incarnations toward a state of spiritual perfection.

Dr. Benjamin taught me that the way to perfect society was to guide people through the levels of development by means of *education*. Therefore, there was, he said, a progression through levels of education.

In 1951, I entered a doctoral program in Education at Columbia University in New York. My advisor there was Doctor Paul Mort. His major interest was the development of society through *eras* or *ages* in pre-history and history. He related eras or ages in human development metaphorically to geologic ages in Earth's development.

I plugged all of this into my evolving religious understanding of a plan for the saving and perfecting of human society. As I worked on my doctoral dissertation, it began to come out as the first draft of what would become my book, *This Dynamic World*. That was not acceptable to Columbia University as a dissertation and so I left New York and reentered public school teaching in Maryland. I installed my family on our farm and pursued my calling as a teacher.

In 1956, I became aware of another input to my ruminating system for helping society. I learned about George King and his *Aetherius Society* in Britain. I noted that, like Paramahansa Yogananda, King had moved himself and his society to southern California, Los Angeles and Santa Barbara. They all seemed to end up in California.

At any rate, as *Wikipedia* says, George King served in the Emergency Fire Service all through the evacuation of Dunkirk and the two blitzes on London – The Battle of Britain and the Reign of Terror from the V-1's and V-2's. This was a man who had prayed for his mother who was ill unto death and said he got a revelation from an angel that his mother would recover and she did.

In 1946, he was 26 years old. So he was my exact same age. I was studying yoga. He was studying yoga as well as other healing arts. I was a school teacher. He was a London taxi driver. I was only contemplating writing my book when he published his manifesto on the right human society entitled *You are Responsible*.

In 1954, when I was back on the farm, George King heard the voice of an *astral being* (he said) that had projected himself from another dimension in the *astral plane*. This *alien* as we call them today said his name was *Aetherius* and his message to George King was "Prepare yourself! You are to become the voice of interplanetary parliament."

George King spent his long life (He died in 1997) developing the *Aetherius Society* to channel instructions for the betterment of mankind from a society of astral people who lived on astral worlds on a completely different astral plane or dimension where they had evolved to a joyous, harmonious, perfected state that served as an example for our development.

AETHERIUS SOCIETY

DR. GEORGE KING

FIGURE 5

This all sounds pretty incredible until we recall our belief in *angels*, heavenly messengers, and also Jesus being the Son of God and coming "down" to us from a world "up" there called "heaven." Also, there is Einstein's hard scientific and mathematical theory of the *space time continuum* which posits that time is a "fabric" that can be "folded," thus making "will" and "was" co-existent with "is" and "are" but not visible to this plane of existence but clearly present on another "wave length" on the "bandwidth" of the fourth dimension.

What Einstein proved and what George King proclaimed are the only rational explanations of prophecy, are they not? George King, Levi Dowling, Paramahansa Yogananda, modern prophets, ancient prophets from the Mayans to Moses (and all the Old Testament prophets), Mohammed, John the Revelator, and Jesus Christ are all somehow spiritually tuned in to perceiving this time fabric where everything is happening now. It is kind of a time tapestry, if you will. *But you have to be spiritual.*

This excited me. It preoccupied me. I wanted to know what they had to say. I wanted to build my utopian society on what they prophesied.

THE WORLD I LIVED IN...THE WORLD I LIVED THROUGH

Also, advanced technology simply exploded all around me. I tried hard to be positive, though it was frightening and painful to watch the world career through violent upheaval and insidious decay. While George King was building the Aetherius Society in Britain, I became a professional educator with the mission of passing on to others what I was learning about life. When the message became insistent enough, I just had to write my book. The history I was living through motivated me.

My fifth horrendous experience was the Cold War (1946-989). Remember, I was the elementary school teacher who taught the kids to "duck and cover," as though under their desks they were safe from the bomb. I could hardly believe my eyes when I saw the great Berlin Wall come tumbling down. There was real hope that a nuclear World War III had been prevented.

My sixth horrendous experience has been watching the prophecies about the Last Days – Christian, Jewish, Muslim, Hindu, astrological, astronomical, geological – come true. There are wars and rumors of wars against terror, against drugs, against poverty, against God, in the name of God. When the wild fires flare, the moon does turn to blood. Scientists foretell the earthquakes, not if, but when. Based on precise measurements, they can say when there will be no polar ice caps. We have the capability to calculate collisions with meteors and we are speculating on what we might do about them.

I line up the Scriptures with the predictions of masters and clairvoyants of the New Age and I learn more about both. I learn about major earth changes in our millennial time. Richard W. Noone, in his book *5/5/2000: ICE: The Ultimate Disaster*, (Harmony House, 1986, p. 53) speaks of the 6,000 year alignment of the planets, due on 5/5/2000. The calendars of the ancient Mayans and Egyptians stop in 2012. Certainly we can do nothing to stop the alignment, but we can live as though we mattered and time didn't.

In the *Gospel According to Matthew*, 17:20, Jesus tells us that "If you have the faith of a grain of mustard seed, you can move mountains." Never has there been a greater need for the youth of the world to come forth in a kind of positive spiritual renaissance. We must harmonize the ethers with thoughts and acts of love. Conflict is not the answer. We must find the *superconscious soul* by losing the *egoist self* in loving service of others. This is the true religion that answers all questions.

We need to make a greater effort to identify those leaders and projects around the world that are moving in positive directions, then pitch in to help them. People must combine spirituality and education into creation of the whole life. The world has hardly begun to realize its potential for good and for our salvation.

My seventh great experience, therefore, was not horrendous but a positive revelation. I like the thought of John White who wrote the book *Pole Shift*. White points out that we are now headed for a terrible pole shift, as predicted by seers *unless* we learn to profit from these predictions and then take immediate action to create conditions which will prevent the predicted catastrophe. The revelations do not foretell what must be. They warn of what may be if we use our freedom to choose evil.

Edgar Cayce

Way back in 1962, a man I regard as a prophet, the late Edgar Cayce, described a *pole shift*. Drawing from 19th and 20th century scholarship, he said that, somewhere around the year 2000, the axis of the earth through the north and south poles would shift. This would, in turn, cause the surface of the earth to move over the molten core.

That movement would, in turn, cause massive climate shift.

Citing his sources, Cayce said that the poles would move because of an over accumulation of ice.

It is 2009. Rather than an *over* accumulation, there is an *under* accumulation of ice at the polls. The weight in the world is the water in the oceans. By the year 2100, say the universities and agencies serving the United States and the United Nations, the waves will lap the shore somewhere between four and twenty feet higher than ever before in human history. Though somewhat different than what Cayce described, he was close to getting it right. There will be climate shift due to earth composition changes. All scientists, of whatever level of credibility, agree that there is, in fact, a pole shift of at least one degree per million years and we are experiencing that now.

By the way, I began to prepare for pole shift back in the 1950's. I was mocked just as Noah was mocked. Now I note with interest all the concern for the Mayan calendar and the prophecies of Nostradamus which predict pole shift in 2012. I see that the matter got Hollywood's attention with the blockbuster in the new "end of the world" genre.

Placing some five to ten billion tons of automobile carbons into the atmosphere each year doesn't help. That must cease if we are to help stop major millennial earth changes.

The world is waking up. There is a positive spirit of acceptance of the need for change and an acceptance of responsibility for our own fate. Positive things can be done if we just put our minds to it. Good or bad, as George King said, *we do it to ourselves.*

GLOBAL WARMING

FOR GOOD OR BAD, WE DO IT OURSELVES

FIGURE 6

I live out in the country where little has changed since the first German settlers came here. Still I caught a vision of a remarkable idea: *a city within a building.*

At my age I am trying to learn about how the "the information society" will not only put *total life* within the home, but those homes can be made complete in all ways. Some of the modern shopping malls indicate the shape of things to come. Now we can *live* within that building, too.

To eliminate the smog, eliminate the car. I think the car should go exactly where the horse and buggy went . . . into antique shops. Would I dare suggest that the airplane go to the same place?

I believe we should stop *taking the physical body to things* and, instead, *take things to people,* materially or virtually. Better yet, don't do either. Learn to *create on the spot* anything that is needed (Remember the "replicator" in the Starship Enterprise?) The human body is a micro universe with endless potentials. Correct me if I am wrong but I think you "young" people call that the internet.

Space? My hunch is this. Isn't it true that we can't get our mineral mechanical spaceships to go faster than the speed of light? That being true, we can't get to the nearest star in a hundred lifetimes, can we? Stop disturbing the ethers with two billion dollar rockets and space ships. Instead, learn to *go within.* After you become *soul aware* and learn to fold time like a blanket, *teleport* to planets, solar systems and galaxies. These astral people on astral worlds in a parallel astral plane of existence... ridiculous? What technological ideas that have been imagined and portrayed in our futurist literature have ever proven to be ridiculous? We blithely say yes, of course, to "transporters" that "beam up" and "beam down" and we say that angels (or aliens) appearing are ridiculous? What close mindedness is this?

And all the time I was writing. I had a draft to show Eleanor Roosevelt in New York in 1951. I had an edition to give to friends in 1962 and 1967. Then *This Dynamic World* came out nationally in 1991. I said then that "This work shall be a drive to raise the consciousness level of all people, and begin to cleanse the world." Long before our Great Depression redux, I said "Mankind needs to become *creators and cleansers,* not *consumers and polluters.*" I referred to this revolution as *the Great Transition,* climbing from level to level in Dr. Benjamin's description of human progression.

From the day when I first pledged to God that I would create something useful from my thoughts and experiences, 64 years have passed. Now I am 92 years old, but I remember everything I have seen and I still believe. The technology that man has made has passed me by, but I am aware of all the things that man has done to and must do with God's creation.

Because so much has happened since 1991 and because I am still here, still seeing, and still thinking, my record must be brought forward to the present if it is to show a way to the future. The Cold War is over, but nuclear proliferation is just beginning. The United Nations is no more or less successful than the League of Nations. We left the industrial age and entered the information age, yet we still fill our environment with ever more and more pollution. We used to be called "One World'ers." Now we have been preempted by the "globalists."

Science journals I have surveyed agree that the human being needs to breathe an atmosphere that is at least 21 % oxygen. When I came home from Europe and, indeed, when I first wrote *This Dynamic World,* the atmosphere of our planet was 21% oxygen *measured by calculations of the whole atmosphere.* As I publish this Second Edition of *This Dynamic World* in 2009, our planetary atmosphere has been recalculated the same way. But calculations of *local* atmosphere in *dense urban centers* taken by air samples show 16% oxygen. Note: 76% of the world's population now lives in dense urban centers. There are some heavy industry sites in China where it is approaching 10%. Human beings cannot live with less than 12% oxygen.

Calculations made 50 years ago when I was young and most of my readers were not born account for industrialization in so-called western civilization, but they do not account for *global* industrialization and the destruction of world serving rain forest in favor of world feeding agriculture.

Greenhouse gases you don't see and particulate ash and smoke you do see increase the destructive part of the atmosphere and decrease the nourishing part. This is just the man made part of the problem. When volcanoes and meteors afflicted the earth 250 million years ago, atmospheric oxygen fell to 12% and the animals of that period were extinguished in what scientists call "the great dying."

Then there are the ice ages with their super storms caused by global warming. Arctic and Antarctic ice melts, cooling oceans, and disrupting the warm currents required for temperate climates.

THE GREAT DYING

FIGURE 7

From 1945 to 1990 we were all judged guilty of intractable conflict and handed down a suspended sentence of death by nuclear war. That nuclear executioner stood over us for 45 years. In 1962, the year of the Cuban missile crisis and the year I first published *This Dynamic World* to my local circle of friends and associates, we came the closest we ever would to global nuclear war.

In those same 60's and 70's, along with many consultants, academics, and career military officers turned historians, Ruth Montgomery predicted World War III for the mid 1980's. As chronicled in such futurist fiction as *1985* by Sir John Hackett and *Red Storm Rising* by Tom Clancy, this, in fact, almost came to pass. However, Reagan persuaded Gorbachev to "tear down that wall" in Berlin and the Soviet Union imploded – out built by America in the nuclear arms race to the point of Soviet economic collapse.

Ruth Montgomery

In the period 1978 to 1982, Ruth Montgomery also predicted that, in the aftermath of World War III or of its equally climactic "cold" war, there would be in the 1990's a "walk-in president" who would have a great impact on the issues that concerned us. She later (but still in the early 80's when Barack Obama was age twenty) revised her prediction to 2008.

The huge anti-climax of the end of the Cold War, incidentally, illustrates a major point in *This Dynamic World*, which I gleaned from the work of Cayce and Montgomery and others. Their prophecies say what will happen *if people continue as they are*. On the other hand, they go on to say, if people exercise their *free agency* and *choose the right*, then the judgment of suffering is lifted from them.

Remember that John the Baptist said "Repent ye. Repent ye. Make your path straight." *This Dynamic World* is a positive statement of hope of what may be if we repent.

At any rate, we did not commit the nuclear crime, God be praised. Therefore, the sentence was vacated... sort of. The modern Russian Commonwealth and the United States still have about 10,000 nuclear warheads each (strategic and tactical). The other nuclear powers (and there are more year by year) have several hundred more. There could be a rogue nuclear attack. Still, we do not have the legacy of global nuclear exchange, thank God. We do, however, have the legacy of global nuclear production, testing, and disposal. We have spent about 300 billion dollars so far on nuclear cleanup and could easily spend 300 billion more – this in a time when our average bank bailout is about 300 billion.

Whether one believes in the Old Testament, the New Testament, the New Age, the Age of Aquarius, or -- like me -- all of the above, prophets, ancient and modern, have shown the signs of the times.

From 1962, when I finished my manuscript and distributed my creation to my own circle, to 1991 when I formally published *This Dynamic World*, I called for a "World Wide Crusade of Biorelativity." I call for it again now in this second edition.

What is *biorelativity?* The term was created by John White in his book, *Pole Shift*, but White was describing something that Edgar Cayce had developed in his study of groups practicing this spiritual process. *Biorelativity* is a development from the concepts and practice of meditation and prayer, elevating those practices from individual to group effort. There are many conventional scientific studies on the efficacy of prayer. When a community prays for a person or prays for a people in trouble, the persons prayed for feel a result and experience a benefit. Blessings are measurable.

Edgar Cayce may have worked with the principle of unified spirits praying for an outcome and John White may have given it a name, but this is a fundamental practice of Christianity. Throughout both old and new testaments and in all statements of the Gospel of Jesus Christ there is reference to the power of prayer to make things happen – both in the lives of individuals and in the lives of groups.

The principle of biorelativity says that if the world community prays for a planetary outcome or prays to avoid a planetary consequence *and* if enough of the world community will repent of sins and errors and work together in corrective actions, then God will "heed the prayer of the righteous" and show how to achieve the good outcome and avoid the bad consequence. This is true with pole shifts, climate shifts, asteroid and meteor strikes, and deferring the end of the world generally. We can change the supposedly predestined future *if we massively do the right thing*. This is biorelativity and this is what I, in these last days, have called a World Wide Crusade for Biorelativity.

From the theology of ancient Egypt to the futuristic New Age Aquarians with every Christian creed in between, we see that these are kingdoms to which we may aspire and toward which we are progressing. There are also dark astral realms to which we may be condemned if we choose evil. The Bible calls these places and states of being heaven and hell. My point of view which I have gleaned from my sources is that we can make heaven or hell here on earth. In the end, after all the great conflicts between good and evil are resolved, earth is where heaven will be -- only purified, perfected, and elevated.

This has been my personal evolution to my hard won understanding. From all that I have gathered comes my version of the Plan of Salvation and Happiness.

CHAPTER TWO
PREMISE AND TESTIMONY

To execute the plan of salvation and happiness, I challenge us to unite in understanding the system of systems of this dynamic world.

I have decided that the movement of our world and of we in it is an example of wave theory. Whenever a mass changes progressively through a series of phases, this sequence of changes can be described visually as a wave. A wave goes through a series of changes until it has come to the end of one wave and the beginning of the next wave. This is one complete cycle of the ongoing wave. This rhythmic change cycle is also called a vibration.

Einstein said that mass and energy are the same thing in different forms. Every mass is changing to energy in rhythmic waves of creation and destruction. It grows. It lives. It decays. It dies. As was said before, this is a dynamic world of mass and energy.

All people that believe in a power higher than man say that this power, called by most, God (though by some, *Enlightenment*), is intelligent and has will. There is general agreement among such people that this intelligent being has a spirit (some say also a human body but definitely a spirit) that can intelligently use all the principles of what we call nature (that is, science and mathematics) to bring order to the universe and make things happens. This ability is power. in this case, the power of God or the "higher power" in the universe.

Having will and being intelligent, this being has used his power to create and guide our world through all the *phases* of all the *cycles* of its existence. This ability and this exercise of will to power we call *consciousness*. As we contemplate how everything works and how we work, we feel that God means well. God has emotions we recognize. God loves us and loves his universal creation. God is good. "And God saw everything that he had made, and, behold, it was very good." (Genesis 1:31)

Taking the character, Satan, the Devil, or Lucifer as a metaphor for a principle or a spirit, people say this is the spirit of *rationalization* of desire for that which is pleasant, but destructive. It is the principle of weak surrender to anything desirable but hurtful to people. It is the opposite of the Golden Rule. It is the opposite of faith, hope, and charity.

In between the actual beings, God and the Devil, or just the principles of good and evil, is Man, the human being. All religions, all philosophies, and all scientific inquiries strive to prove either that Man is predestined, predetermined, or programmed by environment and heredity OR that Man is a free, self-determining, or independent being.

All those who choose free agency and independent function have had to accept the logical conclusion that if one is free, then one is responsible. If one is responsible, then one is accountable for the bad effects of choices on others and on the environment supporting us all. That means a person can be guilty and can be required to face consequences of acts. This also means that people choose to obey or follow an individual, institution, government, tribe, or other association. Followers are individually accountable for their participation in groups.

I choose a right way that is rational, but not a rationalization. I choose a peaceful way that is not weak. I choose a successful way that is not cynically materialistic.

All of this requires consciousness. With respect for the scientific determinists who do not believe in spirit, it is clear from many turning points in history all over the world that people have made choices and their choices made a difference. The existence of human agency is as good a definition as any of consciousness. Human beings are self-conscious. They are conscious of each other and of the world around them. They are conscious of the possibility of spirit or they are conscious of some encounter with spirit. This has led many people everywhere to consciously inquire after and even communicate with God.

We are free to choose and we must choose. We can rely solely on our own human abilities or we can ask for help. We can, if we choose, be guided by the mind and intelligence of God's Consciousness.

In the beginning, God consciously applied his knowledge of how things work to pure spirit (principles, laws, processes, and forms). As a kind of great engineer, he organized matter in accordance with law. Thinking of the law of cycles through stages of being, these materials are a grosser, visible "vibration" while spirit is a more refined vibration. Thus material objects are perceived by human beings (possibly aided by human created instruments) while spiritual objects and humans in a spiritual state can only be seen by a human who resonates with a spiritual *vibration* (is "in the spirit").

We human beings, spirit sons and daughters of God and, therefore, literally brothers and sisters, are the family of man. We are commanded to perfect this world and ourselves. If we do that, we can advance to better worlds and a better life.

Levi Dowling, George King, Ruth Montgomery, and everybody who believes in God appearing to man, angels sent from God to man, that Jesus is the Christ who "went up to Heaven," and in the physical existence of Heaven (or, for that matter, hell) all believe in other worlds and other people than the people of Earth. There are people who insist they have been shown these worlds and these people. Call them prophets, seers, or revelators. Some say that the universe is filled with astral (invisible) planets which are even much larger than physical planets, yet the astral planets are so subtle that they can occupy the same space as the physical universe. Others say that there are other physical planets with other physical humans living on them. Still others say that both of these views are true in that God is the "Master of the Universe" and has caused many worlds to be prepared for all of his children throughout the universe as they progress through the Plan of Salvation.

We now know for a fact that the space from your eyes to the paper from which you are reading is filled with at least 100 radio and television programs, each on a different frequency but very much at peace with one another as these "invisible" but very real things work in the same space. Human beings devised this arrangement as God knew they could if they only would. How great is God.

Man's five-sense perceptions are very limited. The five senses cannot detect total reality. Therefore, man with his present low level of consciousness had to do something to improve his lot. Thus the physical sciences were born, whether they tell the whole story or not. We start there and then grow spiritually to a point where we can use the laws of the universe with a God-like capacity… or not. We can use our knowledge of the laws (physical science) to satisfy our gross appetites and exploit our world for our own gratification. We have that other powerful spirit enticing us with what we want to hear.

This Dynamic world is a book that bears my testimony and expresses my rational *and* spiritual premises and principles to explain how our Earth came to its present situation with all of its problems and all of its potential. The book then applies all of this knowledge to see the future we fear and the future we want. Finally, the book sets out a planetary plan of action that can inspire us to put all our thoughts, energy, and ability together in a community action that will make our lives a heaven on earth instead of a hell on earth.

I have tried to design a method of thinking and reasoning that is so simple that many children can use it effectively. This method uses a study of *eras*, *levels*, and *areas* to point out trends and, indeed, a "Trend of All Trends." The discussion of eras shows the dynamic cycle of progression of the earth. The discussion of levels shows the dynamic cycle of progression of the human being. The discussion of areas shows the dynamic deterioration of life heading toward hell on earth and what exactly we all can do to pull out of this descent into hell and, instead, climb up to a celestial or astral plain of existence to make heaven on earth. I provide a check on all this with a view of *ages* of man specifically.

So the rhythm of life is a cycle of conflict. Aristotle said that all beings, human and otherwise, have an origin, a course along which they are motivated to progress in an attraction (or motivation) toward a goal or end state. There is always a friction or an opposition to the progress of this being towards its goal. Thus, the being tends toward conflict resolution in order to fulfill the measure of its creation. We, the human beings, are told by God (if we can hear God) what our origin was, what our course is, and what our goal is.

The world is dynamic. It is never static. The world progresses in the direction we push it. We, the people, are responsible for what we do to the world and to each other. We can fail, but we need not fail. Our destiny is in our own hands.

These, then, are my premises and my testimony. They tell me my origins, my course, and my goal. I use them to motivate me to help other people. Like so many messengers, I am bursting with ideas on how to bring the prompting of the spirit into practical action.

I have tried for these long decades to keep the fervor and the urgency I felt as a young man spared death for a purpose. I am not an apostle or a prophet. An angel is a heavenly messenger. I do not presume that calling. I do not come from the presence of God. I do come from the presence of the Spirit in me. My system is my own, but I firmly believe that my system was given to me. It is correct and will take us where many organizations and institutions have already said we must go.

I am a parishioner, not a preacher. In politics I am opinionated, not elected. I am a little messenger, but I have a big message. I am only one and yet I am one. Judge the message, not the messenger.

What am I, then? Well, it turns out I am a teacher, a professional educator all of my life. I can teach and you can do. I have explained myself to you, my readers. What do I want to teach you to do?

To use hard, modern terms, I want you to learn the system and then I want you to work the system. Up to now this book has been about me and my statement of belief. Now it becomes about you and what you can do to save yourself and your world. I dare to make this attempt. Do you?

Your first objective is to examine concepts of

➢ Creation and evolution.

➢ Time.

➢ Space.

➢ Conflict.

With this foundation of understanding, you will learn how it all works. You will

➢ learn the progress of the world through *dynamic eras of* being.

➢ learn the progress of the world through *dynamic levels of* being.

➢ learn the progress of the world through *dynamic areas of being.*

In order for you to progress through the arc of your own eras, your own levels, in all of your own areas, you must have a burning testimony of the truthfulness of your understanding of how the universe came to be, who or what rules the universe, how you came to be here, what you are supposed to do here, and where you are going from here.

I have given you my testimony. You now know my system of belief. I believe in reincarnation and astral worlds and living on light. I believe that the alignment of stars dictates the passage of our world from one age to the next. I also believe in one God, who is the spirit and the master soul that rules the universe and is the Heavenly Father of us all. I say that this heavenly father had sons that he sent down from heaven to teach us, to help us, to lead us, and -- if we will obey them -- to save us. Each of these sons of heavenly father sent down from heaven provided us with what I consider to be holy writings or scriptures that explain how the world is and what we are and what we must do.

But that's me. What do you believe? What do you know? Where did you come from? Why are you here? Where are you going?

You may be a devout committed Christian of a very traditional sort. You may believe that Jesus is the Christ, that is to say the "Anointed One." Anointed to be what? Anointed to be the king of the unseen Kingdom of God. You may be sure, as the apostle Peter was sure, that Jesus is the only begotten son of Heavenly Father, and came into this world to be the Savior of the world. You may believe that Jesus is the way, the only way. If you believe these things, then the plan of salvation and happiness for all people is contained in the Gospel of Jesus Christ.

You may be a devout, believing Jew. You may believe that we should "Hear, O Israel, the Lord thy God is one God." You may believe that God covenanted with Abraham that if Abraham would serve the true and living God, then God would give Abraham a posterity that would be as numberless as the stars in the sky and as the sands of the sea shore. You may believe that your people were chosen by God to serve him in obedience to the law. You have the Books of the Law and of the Prophets and of the Kings and of the Chronicles. It is from the Kingdom of Israel that the Messiah will come -- the one anointed to be the Redeemer of Israel. You will, of course, observe the Law of Moses. In doing these things, you will recall the world to its obligation to obey God. That is how you will help save the world... by being a never-ending student and practitioner of the way the universe works as explained by God to Moses, Isaiah, and the others on the mountain, in the Temple, and alone with the words of power.

Perhaps you believe that there is no God but Allah and Mohammed is his prophet. If you submit to the will of God, then upon you will descend the peace of God. You may live in the city, but you live a life as clean as the desert. You know that God is all mighty and that intelligence and power flow from prayer and study of the Holy Writings. You come from the same father Abraham (Ibrahim) as your cousins the Jews. They are children of Israel. You are children of Ismail.

The cruel animal level of today's world makes it hard to remember that Christians, Jews, and Muslims all believe the same things up to Jesus. There they part. Christians say that Jesus was the foretold Messiah and the Savior of the world who came and will come again at the end of the world. Muslims say that Jesus was a prophet but not the Mehdi, the Expected One who will come at the end of the world. Jews are glad that Jesus was one of them, a great Rabbi, a master teacher of the Law, but not the Messiah who will come at the end of the world.

You may come from the east. You may have been raised in or you may, like me, have found the tremendous spiritual power and capability of the eastern religions with their emphasis on spiritual connection and participation with God in the mastery of the environment (your world), time, space, life, and death. More than any scientist, you can manipulate for good matter and energy. You know how to actually *do* things (practice yoga) to better yourself, other people, and the world. You can concentrate on elevating yourself through the levels of personal development (the chakras). You can strive for enough merit to elevate yourself with each life you lead. If you attain the highest level of spirituality, you can travel through space and time by your manipulation of unseen forces. You live on cosmic energy. Your goal is enlightenment. Your goal is to perceive and understand everything. You revere all life. In all your dealings with your fellow people, you seek harmony that will confer on you the Mandate of Heaven.

You may have found a way, as I have tried to do, to put all of these approaches together in one all-embracing system of belief and practice that brings science to religion in a study of the stars, the universe, and the natural forces that are the work of God the Creator. All the approaches talk about the end of an old age and the beginning of a new age. You may have evolved a Gospel of Jesus Christ as one Son of God among many who will usher in a new age of enlightenment and love.

You may even be a humanist. You may look at the universe and our world and see, not God, but man. You may hark to the old Age of Enlightenment with its faith in reason. If so, then all the other approaches are foolishness to you, but, if you are honest (intellectually or otherwise) you will see merit in their results. Perform an experiment upon their words and see if your practical wisdom brings you to the same goals.

What I want is for everybody who reads this book to unite on ends no matter what their means. We cannot agree on reincarnation, astral worlds, resurrection, or the nature of God, but I am praying that we will agree on what we must do to save our planet and ourselves in this frightening time.

My whole purpose in putting this book into your hands is that you will decide to do something about what you have learned. It is my most earnest and righteous desire that you will grasp the plan of salvation and happiness that I am sure is contained here and that you will accomplish it. It is not enough to study it. I challenge you to do it.

IT STARTS WITH YOU. IT IS UP TO YOU.

CHAPTER THREE
CREATION AND EVOLUTION

Astrophysicists and Astrogeologists say that the universe began with a "Big Bang" approximately 14.5 billion years ago. They further describe how gases, solids, and liquids were organized (by whom? Or what? Did they organize themselves?) The resultant minerals became galaxies, stars, planets, and moons. Certain gases became the "building blocks of life." Those building blocks became living cells. These cells absorbed nourishment and excreted waste. They grew and divided. Cells became organisms. Organisms became plants and animals. Over time, plants and animals changed in order to survive. We call this evolution.

Obviously, we are certain that this sequence of events happened on our planet. Statistical analysis shows that the circumstances must be right for the same type of planet all over the universe. It would only be logical to presume that there is a community of worlds across the universe that could and should communicate with us if only a way to do that could be discovered.

One of the first important facts that is known about creation is that there have been different *eras* of creation. Discoveries in geology and paleontology have proven that all was not created simultaneously.

On earth, the past three to five billion years of the earth's existence are divided into five geological ERAS. The five geological eras are: Archeozoic, Proterozoic, Paleozoic, Mesozoic and Cenozoic. Taking the evolution of the universe into galaxies, stars, planets and moons as an era, that makes six eras, or *creative periods* in the formation of the world that we know today.

EVOLUTION & CREATION

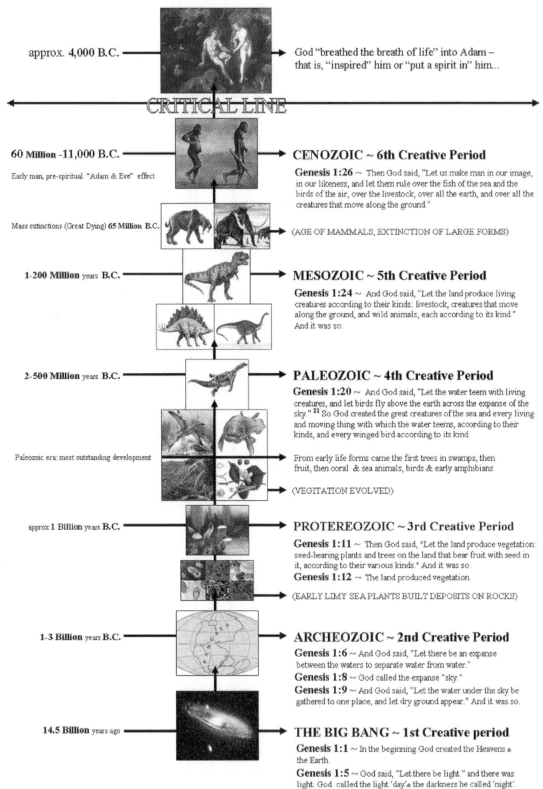

approx. 4,000 B.C. — God "breathed the breath of life" into Adam – that is, "inspired" him or "put a spirit in" him...

CRITICAL LINE

60 Million -11,000 B.C.

Early man, pre-spiritual "Adam & Eve" effect

CENOZOIC ~ 6th Creative Period

Genesis 1:26 ~ Then God said, "Let us make man in our image, in our likeness, and let them rule over the fish of the sea and the birds of the air, over the livestock, over all the earth, and over all the creatures that move along the ground."

Mass extinctions (Great Dying) 65 Million B.C.

(AGE OF MAMMALS, EXTINCTION OF LARGE FORMS)

1-200 Million years B.C.

MESOZOIC ~ 5th Creative Period

Genesis 1:24 ~ And God said, "Let the land produce living creatures according to their kinds: livestock, creatures that move along the ground, and wild animals, each according to its kind." And it was so.

2-500 Million years B.C.

PALEOZOIC ~ 4th Creative Period

Genesis 1:20 ~ And God said, "Let the water teem with living creatures, and let birds fly above the earth across the expanse of the sky." [21] So God created the great creatures of the sea and every living and moving thing with which the water teems, according to their kinds, and every winged bird according to its kind.

Paleozoic era: most outstanding development

From early life forms came the first trees in swamps, then fruit, then coral & sea animals, birds & early amphibians

(VEGITATION EVOLVED)

approx 1 Billion years B.C.

PROTEREOZOIC ~ 3rd Creative Period

Genesis 1:11 ~ Then God said, "Let the land produce vegetation: seed-bearing plants and trees on the land that bear fruit with seed in it, according to their various kinds." And it was so.
Genesis 1:12 ~ The land produced vegetation.

(EARLY LIMY SEA PLANTS BUILT DEPOSITS ON ROCKS)

1-3 Billion years B.C.

ARCHEOZOIC ~ 2nd Creative Period

Genesis 1:6 ~ And God said, "Let there be an expanse between the waters to separate water from water."
Genesis 1:8 ~ God called the expanse "sky."
Genesis 1:9 ~ And God said, "Let the water under the sky be gathered to one place, and let dry ground appear." And it was so.

14.5 Billion years ago

THE BIG BANG ~ 1st Creative period

Genesis 1:1 ~ In the beginning God created the Heavens & the Earth.
Genesis 1:5 ~ God said, "Let there be light." and there was light. God called the light 'day'& the darkness he called 'night'.

FIGURE 8

In 1651, James Ussher, Bishop of Armagh and Primate of the (Protestant) Church of Ireland, published his famous *Chronology* of the history of the world, in which he said that the world was created on the 23rd of October in 4004 B.C., probably at about nine o'clock in the morning.

American playwrights Jerome Lawrence and Robert Edwin Lee had a lot of fun with this in their play *Inherit the Wind*. Scientists from Darwin forward completely disregard the scholarship of the good Bishop. Consider, however, that maybe what Ussher meant was that the six periods of the creation of the world *ended* 4004 years before the birth of Christ. And is not a "day" sometimes a metaphor for an age or an *era*? After all, everything else in the Bishop's chronology works out pretty well. Indeed, the end of prehistory with no written record and the beginning of written history is somewhere between 3000 and 4000 years before Christ, depending on what society you are looking at.

Everything described by Darwin and all scientists since put the *conclusion* of the six great creative periods that brought our world into being right on time for Bishop Ussher's chronology. Thus, the universe and our world in the universe were "created" by the organization of matter and energy over six great creative periods ("days" if you will), followed by a "day" of rest while God contemplated his creation and executed the Plan of Salvation (and Happiness) by "transplanting" his spirit children into appropriately prepared human beings for life here on Earth.

Cannot all believers agree that the account of creation in the *Book of Genesis*, like all the rest of the *Bible*, is the word of God and historically accurate *as far as it is translated and interpreted correctly*? After all, did not the *Old Testament* particularly pass through the hands of the scribes of Moses and of the kings of Israel, the rabbis of Alexandria, the Latin and Greek Church fathers, and worthies like Bishop Ussher and, finally, those of his colleagues who labored at the command of King James to give us the *Bible* that we use today?

Can the solution of the whole creation conundrum be this simple?

THE TREND OF ALL TRENDS AND THE CRITICAL LINE

At any rate, more things are unknown than known about those distant "days" in the history of the earth, but we know enough to see the *trend* and we can establish the basic characteristic of the *trend of all trends* as it applies to the eras of creation.

My purpose in charting trends is always to find the *critical line* between the evolution of material things and the spiritual progression of human things. Then, when we line up all trend charts, each with its critical line between material and spiritual, we can see the Trend of All Trends from the material past to the spiritual future.

What do we learn from this chart of trends of the Earth's Eras? Since by "Man" we mean spirit son of Man of Holiness as described above, we can see that the Trend of All Trends of the Eras of Earth shows us that this Man no more came from animals than animals came from plants. The material realm constantly changes. The Soul never changes. Only mind and body change.

The Trend of All Trends was established by the Creator of the Universe Himself, during billions of years of change and growth. Most of the mineral level of being was created first and is, therefore, the first level of being. Plants were largely created second, and are called the second level of being. Animals were largely created third and are called the third level of being. Mankind was largely created fourth and is called the fourth level of being. Their advancement to spiritual beings was largely created fifth and is called the fifth level of being. This trend of all trends is the trend upwards toward the spiritual level of being. The term *created* should not be placed entirely in the past tense, since creation never ends as long as the manifest being exists.

Most well informed people seem to believe that the solar system, during this life cycle, has about another five billion years to change. Then the supernova stage will be reached, and the materials dissolved for use in the birth of a future solar system, and another ten billion year solar life cycle. Since our solar system now contains heavy metals, it is believable (manifest?) that the present solar system was once part of a past solar system. That is, the materials came from a past supernova.

This means that the entire creation cycle of our planet at least, maybe of our solar system, maybe of our galaxy, and maybe, even, of our universe is one phase of one cycle of a *cycle of cycles*! How great is God!

CHAPTER FOUR

TIME

We are considering trends seen in the use of time within the trend of creation, but we also see that the theory of evolutionary trends in creation requires an organizing intelligence *who knows what to do because he has already done it*. It also requires an organizing intelligence *who knows what is going to happen because he can see the future*. In fact, seeing the future would seem to require visiting the future. But how can a person visit a place in a time that does not exist yet? There is only one way. The future (and, presumably, the past) *exists at the same time as the present*. Thus, time is an *illusion* of people living in a material world, who must rely on past memory to calculate future effects of present choices.

Earth, Sun & Moon

This is too hard for us. Human beings that we are, we live our lives on our planet *linearly* through time. This is our *frame of reference*. Anything else we don't understand and assign to God. But God seems to want us to understand. We feel prodded to learn how things work. We have enquiring minds.

Searching for understanding, we return to our wave theory approach to the rhythm of life.

We look at the time periodic cycles that we call "normal". We understand our solar and lunar cycle. We know that our earth travels once around our sun for each time period we call a year. Our solar year has 12 lunar months.

For each time period we call a month, our moon travels once around our earth. Our month takes 28, 29, 30, or 31 days. The time it takes for earth to rotate once is one of our 24 hour days.

All life on earth has biological or circadian rhythm. All living beings have a time of day, of month, and of the year to awaken, to arise and be active, to grow, to shed, to sleep and be dormant. Every living organism on earth has a cycle of respiration. We inhale; we exhale. We ingest; we digest; we excrete.

If we meditate on these periodic cycles, we can become serene and focused on our healthy routines. If, however, we want to break through to an understanding of the trend of all trends regarding the eras of the life of the earth and the eras of our lives, and if we want to cross over that critical line between the material life and the spiritual life, then we must progress further in our understanding of the great rhythmic cycles of the cosmos.

Milky Way/Galaxy

Not only is the moon in orbit around the Earth, and the Earth in orbit around the sun but also our sun is in orbit around the center of our galaxy. To put it another way, our galaxy slowly, majestically rotates once every 25,000 of our solar years. There is more. Our universe of galaxies is consistently, measurably, and predictably expanding outward from its center. This expansion is the outward momentum of all matter in the universe launched by the famous "Big Bang" that began the universe.

As all of these cycles progress through their time periods, sensitive observers here on earth have learned to predict the path of planets and stars relative to each other. This gives rise to our concept of constellations. Cataloging and analyzing constellations and planets for their value as explanations and predictors of *physical* events is *astronomy*. Cataloging and analyzing constellations and planets for their value as explanations and predictors of *human* events is *astrology*.

All reasonable people in the world accept the validity and usefulness of astronomy. Many reasonable people in the world do *not* accept the validity and usefulness of astrology.

As with the supposedly ridiculous Bishop Ussher, however, are not astrologers trying to get at something spiritual, which can be proven in other ways?

For instance, astronomers say that our sun's orbit around the galaxy is elliptical. As we learned, Astrologers say that the two points of the orbit when our sun is at its closest to the center of the galaxy are ages of enlightenment for people here on earth. They also say that the two points of the orbit when our sun is at its farthest from the center of the galaxy are dark and threatening ages.

Astronomers and astrologers agree that our solar system is approaching the midpoint of the galactic orbit when we are getting as close to the center of the galaxy as we have ever been during the history of mankind. Astrologers say we are leaving behind the Age of Pisces, which is a dark unsatisfactory age. They say we are entering the Age of Aquarius when all the stars and planets are aligned in a positive and beneficial way.

This would seem to correspond with the apocalyptic end of our world as we know it predicted by both the Old and New Testaments of the Bible. Following that, the Jews say the Messiah will come, the Muslims say the twelfth and final Mahdi ("Expected One") will come, and Christians say the Messiah, the Christ, will come again.

Interestingly, the ancient Aztec, Toltec, and Mayan Native Americans have a God named *Quetzcoatl,* the "feathered serpent." His name signifies that he is a God of the land and comes through the air (bird feathers for flying but a serpent on the ground). Quetzcoatl is a bearded white man who came to the people, blessed and taught them, and promised to come back to save them. The Mesoamerican people revered Quetzcoatl as their savior and also as the creator of the earth. The Mayans call the same God Kukulcan. (See *Quetzalcoatl: Toltec and Aztec God, The Plumed Serpent's Role As the Creator Sky-God,* Henry Ramsager, Jan 1, 2008)

It should be remembered that Mayan astronomy as well as astrology was very advanced. The Mayans predict that the "astral cycle" of our sun around our galaxy will put us in position for the end of one age and the beginning of the next in our year 2012. This will be the end of the world as we know it and the opening of a new world or way of life. The astronomical and astrological observations of other cultures say the same thing. Ancient Egyptians, the Renaissance prophet, Nostradamus, and the Freemasons, using what they believe is knowledge from the Temple in Jerusalem, all predict the same thing.

Furthermore, astrologers and mystics generally, both East and West, believe that this astral cycle is an evidence of an astral universe coexisting with the known universe but on a different "vibration." This astral universe or higher astral plane, with its astral worlds and astral people coexists with the universe we experience in time and space. According to this scheme, astral people can project themselves into our universe. They can, if you will, "appear" to us and help us.

To Christians, this sounds a lot like the Spirit World and the spirit sons and daughters of Heavenly Father (and Heavenly Mother?) who come from there. It sounds a lot like guardian angels, the better angels of our nature, heavenly messengers (Greek: evangelus), and "Angels we have heard on high, singing sweetly o'er the plain." To put it yet another way, people who haven't been born and people who have died are right next to you, only on the other side of what has been called a veil. They are in the *Spirit World*, which is a spiritual version of this world. When you die, your spirit can go through that veil and be with the people you love and the people you always wanted to meet, but only if you are or are genuinely trying to be spiritual.

We learned about consciousness. If we can be spiritual enough to comprehend this astral or spiritual level of existence, we connect with the wisdom and power of a mass, group *Superconsciousness*.

Just by the way, remember the Magi, the three wise men, "we three kings of orient are," who predicted the birth of Christ with a lineup of planets that would appear as a bright superstar, hovering over the birthplace of the Savior of the world? Well, they were Zoroastrian astrologers!

You may draw back at these meanderings of some old professors, but consider the meanderings of Albert Einstein, Richard Feynman, Steven Hawking, and other pioneers (those who go on ahead *in time!*) of the Theories of General Relativity, Special Relativity, and Quantum Mechanics. (See Albert Einstein, *Relativity*, 1952. See Steven Hawking, *Cosmology from the Top Down*, 2003)

Einstein concluded (concludes?) that *time is a "fabric."* This fabric can be "folded" until, if a being could be found who could do it, all parts of the fabric could be experienced at the same time. What humans (and, indeed, animals) see as a linear progression of events in places over a period of time is, in reality, a giant "mural" of all events in all places at the same time.

In the *Book of Exodus* in the *Old Testament* (Exodus CH 30-33), when Moses has led the people deep into Sinai, he goes up to the mountain top to speak with God while the people camp below. Moses is taught and counseled by God for a long time. The people get restless and think he has abandoned them. The people force Aaron to make them a golden calf to worship in sensual, Canaanitish ways.

Meanwhile, Moses is getting instruction in how the universe works and how mankind ought to live. Moses comes down the mountain with *two* tablets written on by God *on both sides* (Exodus 32:15-16). It is a wealth of knowledge and commandments, far more than "the ten commandments."

Moses comes down, sees the people having what amounts to an orgy around the golden calf, is furious, and casts down the tablets. Moses fights a brief civil war, recalls the people to the Lord, begs God to not destroy the people, and is called back up on the mountain. There, in Exodus 33:19-23, God shows Moses "...his glory" (his creation?). God says, "I will make all my goodness pass before thee." There are many Christians who believe that God showed Moses this "mural" of the "fabric" of time. God showed Moses all events, in all places, at all times *simultaneously* which is how God sees things. He then gave Moses the Ten Commandments as a lesser law that the people could live at their lower level of spiritual attainment.

This reward for righteousness given to Moses is what makes him a *prophet.* This ability to see that mural of that fabric is what makes a prophet. This is what prophecy is. The key is, a person must rise to the spiritual level of being in order to have a chance at that. At the human level, Einstein could discover it, but he couldn't do it.

What have we learned? We are materialistic human beings living in the "real world." Reality *manifests* itself continually with forces that set in motion objects in accordance with wills. We are surrounded by *manifest beings.* However, we want more. We don't want to die. We want to live forever. We want the people we love to live forever. We want our relationships with the people we love to live forever. We have enough desire for these things that we can exercise a particle of faith in the existence of spirit. Sometimes, when we are confronted with life and death, good and evil, God and the devil, we feel our spirit inside us. We want to know where our spirit came from and where it is going. We want to know what we have to do to get where we want to go.

Putting ourselves on the chart, we are motivated to progress from a material understanding of manifest phenomena to a spiritual understanding of as yet *unmanifest* phenomena. Understanding the fabric of time and its relation to prophecy of other worlds is the way we do that.

CHAPTER FIVE

SPACE

When I showed my first draft of *This Dynamic World* to Eleanor Roosevelt in 1951, there were 2.593 billion people on our planet.

I first published *This Dynamic World* in 1962. In that year, there were 3.139 billion people on our planet.

In 1991, I published *This Dynamic World* nationally and there were 5.359 billion people on our planet.

Now, in this 2009 Second Edition of *This Dynamic World*, I see there are 6.783 billion people on our planet.

The surface area of Planet Earth remains what it has always been, 510,072,000 square kilometers of which 148,940,000 square kilometers is land. That is an earth's surface that is 30% land and 70% water.

So:

In 1951, there were 1.74 humans per square kilometer of land.

In 1962, there were 2.11 humans per square kilometer of land.

In 1991, there were 3.60 humans per square kilometer of land.

In 2009, there were 4.55 humans per square kilometer of land.

THERE IS ROOM IF WE SPREAD OUT

YEAR OF STATISTICS RECORDED	HUMANS PER SQUARE KILOMETER
1951	1.74 humans
1962	2.11 humans
1991	3.60 humans
2009	4.55 humans

FIGURE 9

The human population of Earth is increasing logarithmically, but even at that rate of growth, it will be a long time before the population of the entire land area of the Earth is as densely packed as the population of a modest city today.

Of course, another factor to be considered is *available* land. There are areas of the Earth that are not only unattractive but unsuitable for human habitation by any but a small community of extremely adapted people (Arab Bedouins, African Bushmen, Australian Aborigines, and the like). One entire continent – Antarctica – is completely uninhabitable by any but specially equipped and trained humans who are, in effect, on another world as certainly as if they were establishing a Mars or Moon colony.

The good lands are being encroached upon by the bad lands as climate change accelerates desertification. Climate change caused by global warming melts polar ice and causes Earth's oceans to rise. This floods coastal land which has always been the most densely populated part of the Earth. Of course, (other than on habitable islands) there cannot be the usual communities and countries out on the sea.

We are agricultural beings. We have to be. There are far too many of us to be hunter gatherers in modern times. Even if we wanted to "live off the land," our ancestors hunted and fished and picked almost all of the Earth's bounty. Now we can't use enough fertilizer or enough pesticides and herbicides and certainly can't get enough water to raise enough food for all of us. Also, as noted above, climate change means drought and desertification so there is less water and less useful soil. If we want to eat meat and wear hides and if there is not near enough game to feed an actual modern community, then we must do animal husbandry as a branch of agriculture which means even less water, soil, and crops for us and more for the animals.

FIGURE 10

Increasingly, the inhospitableness of the countryside forces us into urban areas that are unplanned and unable to provide for huge dense masses of people. The literal drying up of planetary resources and the encroachment of the sea upon the land makes for horrendous and inhumanly vicious conflict over scarce resources. This doesn't even begin to take into account the hoarding of mineral wealth and the conflict over energy resources for industrial and residential purposes.

This is animals living on plants fighting over minerals.

Conventional economic and political thinking is that the human race is too big and the Earth is too small. We are on a path of mathematically inevitable exhaustion of planetary resources. We are doomed to war, disease, and starvation in a literally and metaphorically poisonous environment.

In the late 18th century, Adam Smith published his *Wealth of Nations* as the explanation of capitalism and free enterprise. He talked of government keeping "hands off," *laissez faire* in French. He said that individual ambition and desire to gain would work as an "invisible hand" to stimulate development and create wealth. He was the apostle of abundance and he inspired the industrial revolution.

In the early 19th century, Robert Malthus published his *Essay on the Principle of Population* as a reality check on the unbridled excess of Anglo-European development with its tremendous population increase. Malthus did the math on population and resources and came to the inescapable conclusion that population must not increase. If it did, there would be an end to the world as he knew it. He gave us expressions like "Malthusian dilemma" and "Malthusian catastrophe." He died in 1834 but he could point, in his lifetime to the upheavals of the Irish potato famine and two French Revolutions (1789 and 1830) as justification of his theories. He didn't live to see it but his theories predicted the massive pan-European Revolution of 1848. He was the apostle of scarcity and he inspired the doctrine of population control.

People who were cheered by Adam Smith and appalled by Robert Malthus saw a solution to the problem in emigration and immigration – population shift comparable to today's climate shift. European and British population flowed to America, Canada, South Africa, and Australia. Newcomers to new lands could "spread out" as the Americans like to say.

Also, long before America was "realizing westward" as the American poet, Robert Frost, had it, while the Spanish Empire was sending conquerors, settlers, and missionaries to all Latin America, the Russian Empire sent conquerors, settlers, and missionaries following the receding Mongol Empire into the Eurasian landmass, what the geopolitician Erich Haushofer called the "heartland of the world."

Moreover, the Chinese Empire moved south and east from its northern origins, absorbing and assimilating all people in its path, like a human glacier.

Just as *The Bible*, the Mayans, Nostradamus, and all the others predict, human societies, their nation states, and empires of associated states either filled up or drained of resources huge areas. Population growth provided the manpower to cultivate and otherwise develop these vast new regions, but, inevitably, Malthusian certainties took over. People consumed everything the land provided and needed more. Our system of understanding will show us how we can make more.

The eras, levels, and areas of Creation taught us not to be afraid of time. The Plan of Salvation is also the Plan of Happiness. Clearly the history of the planet Earth is linear. However, it is like a carpet which is unrolled. Once fully unrolled, with its entire surface exposed, the carpet may be rolled back up. It may be folded back onto itself. Once laid out, its entire surface may be seen simultaneously. We will be happy when we cross the critical line between the non-spiritual part of the Human Era and humanity's Spiritual Era. We will be good stewards of the Lord over his creation when we have a spiritual perspective on all time. As our homely expression has it, we will "use our time wisely" with good "time management."

Even though all of the prophetic predictors of what is going to happen in time to come say that we will experience cataclysm, those same prophetic predictors all agree that it is God's will (or, at any rate, the right thing to do) to live spiritually, that is, lovingly, positively, helpfully, happily. If we do this, we live in God's permanent presence without regret and without fear. We make time work for us and appreciate the spirit world toward which we are going.

If we can transcend human nature and cross the critical line in the eras, levels, and areas of creation from what the Bible calls "fallen man" to a humanity that is spiritual, then we can regard space with as much serenity as time.

The first thing to note is that the higher the level of creation, the smaller the physical size.

MINERAL ERA OF SPACE

In the Mineral Era, everything takes up a huge space. Mountains, --both on land and underwater, -- are massive and can provide the spines of whole continents. As we have noted, water, both salt and fresh, is 70% of the earth's surface. Deserts are huge. Plains or steppes are huge.

PLANT ERA OF SPACE

In the Plant Era, everything takes up less space. A plant, even a lofty ancient tree, is smaller than a boulder or a cliff. The great expanse of interior Russia that we call Siberia is comprised of *tundra* and *taiga*. The tundra is frozen Arctic grassland. The taiga is boreal forest (small low trees well spread out in grassland, with numberless ponds and lakes). Standing in Siberia and looking north, an old Russian proverb says, "Nobody knows where the taiga ends." The truth is that the taiga ends on the shore of the Arctic Ocean, where the polar ice cap begins. It then continues down the other side of the North Pole, filling northern Canada.

But the truth is that, even when we add together the great evergreen forests of Canada and the United States, the Amazon rain forest, the equatorial African rain forest, and the jungles of Southeast Asia, we have not accounted for nearly as much area as we see in the Andes Mountains, the Himalayan Mountains, the Ural Mountains and the various mountain ranges of Southwest and South Asia. Then there is desert that, in an earlier era, was plant covered savanna. Such areas today are rocks and sand with molten plants underneath.

An evidence of the fact that mankind is an order of being distinct from every other life form on earth is the way that man can actually make the earth go backward to an earlier era. It could be said that there is regression from the Plant Era back to the earlier Mineral Era.

Consider that, today, desert is increasing. Across North Africa stretches the world's largest hot desert, covering 9,000,000 square kilometers. We call it the Sahara, because the Arabic word for desert is saḥ'ra. It is Saḥ'rā al-Kubra, "The Greatest Desert." The Greatest Desert is getting even larger. It spreads to the south year-by-year. In Central Asia, the Gobi Desert eats its way eastward ever deeper into China.

Consider that there were huge deciduous forests in the eastern United States and in Western Europe. Agricultural man cleared away most of that for crops, homes, and fuel. That same harvesting and clearing of trees is happening now in South America, Africa, and Asia. It is being said that the state of Montana is the "Saudi Arabia of coal." There are voices that want to literally flay or skin Montana, revealing the black treasure underneath. Every tree in Montana would become lumber or firewood.

If this sounds too preposterous to ever happen, consider the fate of the Athabasca Wilderness Area of northern Alberta in Canada. Huge strip mines have peeled away the boreal forest, revealing the black tar sands underneath.

So plants are smaller than minerals. Climate change, caused by both humans and nature, can increase mineral dominated areas and decrease plant covered areas. The combination of climate change and human activity can even return the earth to the Mineral Era.

What about plants in the water? Floating ocean plankton generates half of the world's oxygen. Near enough to shore to capture the necessary sunlight are forests and gardens of underwater plants. All of this bounty is too small to be apprehended by humans.

Thus we see that the earth progresses from Mineral Era to Plant Era with a smaller number of plants in a smaller area of plant life, accounting for a greater impact on the earth than the larger mineral formations and areas.

ANIMAL ERA OF SPACE

Continuing through the eras, animals are smaller still. The Animal Era is distinguished by animal species who adapt themselves to every kind of plant and mineral environment.. Billions of insects are invisible in the forest or grassland. Billions of birds feed on billions of insects and nest in billions of plants and rocks. Billions of water creatures feed on other billions of water creatures without appreciably affecting the water volume of the planet.

There has also been a decrease in the physical size of animals. The huge dinosaur is gone. The mammoth has become the elephant. The pterodactyl has become the Eagle. The giant sloth has shrunk down to the giant short faced bear, thence to the grizzly bear and on down to the little bitty black bear. The giant pelagic shark is succeeded by the great white. The whale, the buffalo and horse have been pushed back. The cow, sheep and goat will probably be next.

HUMAN ERA OF SPACE

Enter pre-spirit inhabited mankind. These are the Homo sapiens that evolved from primates. These are the smallest post-primate mammals living in kinship groups comparable to herds. Even here we see an evolution to a smaller size. Neanderthals are smaller than Cro-Magnon's. Modern humans are smaller than Neanderthals. The human male that received the Spirit son of Heavenly Father was smaller and more delicate still.

The *critical line* between the eras of space is the line dividing the Human Era of Space from the Spiritual Era of Space. Therefore, it is interesting to note that the human level of creation is one of the two very small things in physical size. In fact, like the birds and the bugs and the fish, it is relatively invisible to an inspector of the surface of the planet. It has been reported many times the only man-made feature on our earth visible from space is the Great Wall of China. That, of course, is the result of human manipulation of the large products of the Mineral Era.

SPIRITUAL ERA OF SPACE

The spiritual level above the human level is invisible to currently very human man. To put it another way, the human level approaches the spiritual state as the level of *consciousness* is raised.

In fact, ALL things tend to take up less space. That is, they intrude upon each other less as they approach their spiritual goals.

LEVELS OF SPACE

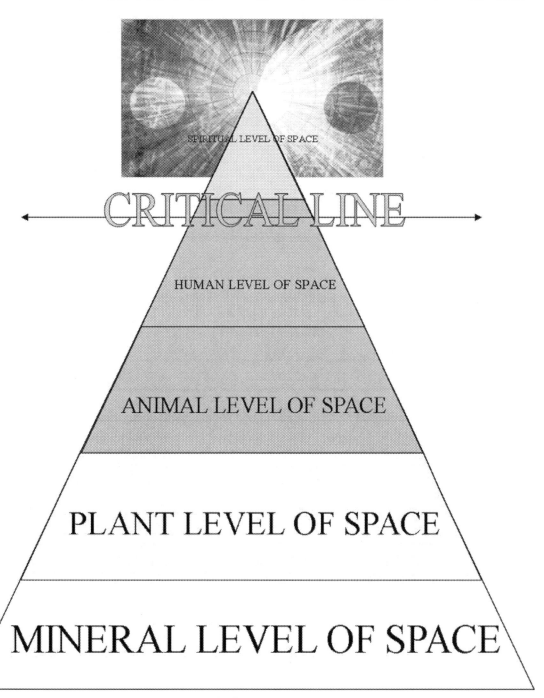

SPIRITUAL LEVEL OF SPACE

CRITICAL LINE

HUMAN LEVEL OF SPACE

ANIMAL LEVEL OF SPACE

PLANT LEVEL OF SPACE

MINERAL LEVEL OF SPACE

FIGURE 11

The *trend* of the eras of the use of space is a trend of *decreasing physical size*. During the billions of years of creation, most things became smaller as they evolved "upward." One reason for this might be that the miles of minerals, for example, evolved from a volume which was much larger than its present size. As the earth continues to cool today, it also continues to get smaller. Thus, the surface tends to wrinkle, forming mountains. The earth is not likely to get too much smaller during its remaining five billion year life span, at which time it will be dissolved along with the sun in the process of supernova. As the earth's gravity tends to pull its satellites back to it, so the sun tends to pull its planet-satellites back. Also, each pound of matter turned into energy reduces the size of the earth. The sun also gets smaller at the rate of four million tons per second, as the hydrogen fusion process continues to consume matter to make light and heat.

We see that the trend of the eras teaches us about managing time. We must live spiritually, that is, timelessly. Only the present is real. Past and future are illusions until we cross over into the spirit world where we can see all time in one instant.

What does the trend of the eras say about managing space? There is plenty of room for all of the people that there are or ever will be up to the end of our natural span of time here on this earth *IF* we regard our use of space and our use of time *spiritually*. What is the critical spiritual statement about neighbors? Jesus said (quoting the Scriptures as he always did), "Love thy neighbor as thyself." (Matthew 5:43; Leviticus 19)

If we would be spiritual beings, we must consider the earth to be a living, breathing, growing, changing organism. We live on it. We live in it. We travel over it. Native American people say the earth is our mother. Polynesian people say, we are the children of the land. The earth nurtures us. We must nurture the earth.

We must leave behind us forever the age of fossil fuels. We must stop burning things in the air to make our energy. No more fire energy – unless it is fire in a faraway place. The sun is our ultimate energy source. We reach through the space time continuum to re-grasp what our ancestors knew about the sun. We use the sun's rays themselves and we use the fusion principle by which the sun works. We use the wind derived from heated and cooled air currents. We use moving water to be sure but we make sure that our atmosphere lets sun heat out as smoothly as it let it in.

We cannot do these things immediately, but we must begin immediately to do these things. We were warned years ago, generations ago. Now we are confronted with a self caused end of the world due to global warming and the resulting climate chaos for which God is not responsible.

We begin our exit from the age of fossil fuels by obeying the laws which we have made for ourselves. We return power to environmental protection agencies that were stripped of power and we instruct them to enforce laws that have been circumvented. We insist on emission standards that can only be met by the use of reformulated gasoline, natural gas, biofuels, gas-electric hybrids, fuel cells, and fusion engines.

We increase the effectiveness of catalytic converters and we use that technology in "smoke stack industries." We put coal catalyst carbon filters in smoke stacks which route the filtered CO_2 not into useless carbon sequestration tanks but into enhanced oil and methane recovery systems. These use pollution controls to blow more clean fuel to the surface.

We bend smoke stacks over so the dirty smoke is going around in a horizontal, artificial tornado. Squirt some liquid fuel (probably natural gas) into the smoke and light it. Burn the smoke. The additional combustion drives an electric power plant which provides electricity to the coal fired industrial plant or more electricity from a coal fired power plant. It is an afterburner for a smoke stack.

CLEAN ENERGY

FIGURE 12

We reduce hydrocarbon emissions by 90% in three years. For 30 years we have said oh, that can't be done; that can't be done; that can't be done. We don't have the technology yet. The technology is coming. When the technology arrives, if it is cost effective, then we will do it. Now it is the end of the world that is coming. We refuse to obey our laws, and God's, at the cost of our lives.

We instruct our government to legislate emissions standards for industry as well as for transportation that would inevitably bring about a 90% reduction in three years. After mandating standards, we instruct our government to assist industry in taking fossil fuel use to its highest possible level of cleanliness and efficiency.

Then we instruct our government to make laws that will motivate conversion to a post-fossil fuel economy.

Tell people what they have to do and then help them do it.

The government can make you do things, but it cannot make you think things. Even with mandates and assistance, we will exit from the age of fossil fuels only when we change our minds.

Consider that this is a time when large parts of the earth's surface make no food for humans. This is a time when large numbers of humans cannot get food. Food is given to them or they die. Frequently the gifted food is stolen from them and they die. In this time of global want, 60% of Americans are obese. These Americans have decided that they will only eat what pleases them. What pleases them is a certain savor, a certain richness, a certain stimulation, a certain satisfaction. They only eat food that is white. They eat white sugar, white flour, white potatoes, white oil, and white fat. They eat food that comes out of a factory. They will not eat food that comes out of the ground. The odd thing is that food that comes out of the ground has much more savor and richness than food that comes out of a factory, but they don't believe that and they won't try it. They will not change their minds. Some have said that everybody is addicted to something. This is carbohydrate addiction.

It is the same with personal transportation powered by internal combustion engines burning fossil fuel. Before the age of the automobile, the ultimate in transportation as personal identity and sensual pleasure was the man on the horse. A knight rides a horse.

A gentleman rides a horse. A rich man rides a horse. A frontiersman rides a horse. An independent man who has liberty rides a horse. When a man has proven his manly worth by demonstrating competence with a horse, he can advance to his own wheeled vehicle pulled by his own horses. Now he is at liberty to convey his family and his property wherever and whenever he and they want to go. Only for long journeys, transcontinental journeys, does a man submit to the need for amazing but somehow demeaning public transportation.

As it was with horses and railroads, so it is with automobiles and airplanes. Here's how I described it in 1962, with updates for 1991.

> "In these semi-dark days of air pollution and the horrific storms they cause, man still seems to joyfully devour his own, as one animal joyfully devours another animal at mealtime. Every day in America man's almost 200 million "Autodragons" smack their four wheeled lips on some 100 juicy human steaks, while the rest of the herd bask in the "good-life" founded upon a system of "Autodragon" transportation. Man

shines, polishes and perfects his "Autodragons" with a religious fervor. He sings his daily hymns of praise to it over radio and television with a zeal not equaled in the worship of his God. In reality, this is a mineral level of worship and religion.

Those individuals who are lucky enough to escape the feeding habits of some 200 million "Autodragons" each year (some 45 to 50 thousand are not so lucky), are about as unconcerned of the fact that they could be next, as one daisy is unconcerned about the fact that it might be next in a Fall bouquet. Such shocking unconcern for one's own self, as well as for one another, is not only not on the spiritual level; it is almost not on the human or animal levels. A pack of wild dogs would show about the same concern for the safety of one another."

Harsh and heedless, my statement is descriptive and I stand behind it in 2009.

The glamour is leaving the automobile and the airliner. The new patrician ride is clean, speedy, safe, quiet, light rail, commuter rail and cross-country "bullet" trains. The generation after that will be movement with magnets on cushions of air.

We must return to transcontinental rail travel, but at speeds of 200 miles an hour. In a transcontinental journey, we can then dispense with two hours wasted in each of three airports. When we travel this way, we can have food and accommodations enroute that are an extension of home and office. Air travel would become one leg flights for travelers with a real need for that speed. The "hub system" would be obsolete.

The real usefulness of air travel would be, as it is now, *transglobal* (or overseas) travel. Here the largest planes use the largest airports to efficiently carry the largest loads of freight and people. Even here, however, the old way is making a comeback.

In 2009, the largest cargo aircraft in the world is the Antonov-225. It weighs 660 tons of which 300 tons are cargo. A very small, ocean going cargo ship weighs 4000 tons of which 2000 tons are cargo. There are super tankers of 200,000 tons burthen. Cruise ships don't count as they are recreation, not transportation. There are nineteen ocean liners transiting the world's oceans and seas today bigger than aircraft carriers and built to comply with the 2010 Safety of life at Sea (SOLAS) Regulations. Could there be more built with service comparable to rail and air? On the Titanic, we would call them "Third Class" and "steerage." Today, we would call them "business" and "economy."

As with the railroads, maritime commerce is the only way to efficiently flow mass quantities of goods from all suppliers to all customers. Just as a passenger train carries in a few railcars extending perhaps a quarter of a mile as many people as would fill cars and trucks jamming several miles of multi-lane freeway, so does a modest sized, hard working ship carries more people or more cargo than a hundred of the largest cargo or passenger aircraft.

Meanwhile, on land, the interstate highway system would not be desired for routine transcontinental personal travel or for the over the road transport of freight. Long haul freight by rail is already making a comeback. The new hub system would use distribution centers in all urban centers (They already exist). Freight trains bring the goods to the distribution center and trucks spread it out from there to the receivers of the goods. Rail passengers get off at the rail "hub" of their choice and rent a car to complete their journey.

Think of a ten lane freeway in rush-hour. Calculate the number of cars and trucks packed into a ten mile length of that freeway. With the vast majority of these vehicles carrying one person, figure how many human beings occupy that ten mile length of that ten lane road. Now put all those people in a train. With much more legroom, shoulder room, and headroom enough to stand up, how much space would these people take up riding along on their train? How long is the train? ...a half mile? ...a quarter mile? How wide is a rail right-of-way compared to a freeway right-of-way?

In the metropolitan areas, driving and parking a car would be uncool. Cool in the city is fun trolleys and street cars (technical name: light rail), commuter rail (including elevated, magnet powered, air cushioned, monorails), bending "slinky" buses emitting no diesel smoke. Finally, there is the anti-obesity bicycle.

Nevertheless, America is still America to the very end. A man can still have his pickup truck in the great expanses of rural America where trains and planes and little cars cannot go. A man can still carry his family in an elegant sedan. The mystique of the mounted man and the class of the "surrey with the fringe on top" can go on. It's just that, for personal transportation, we still have the internal combustion engine but burning reformulated gasoline, natural gas and biofuels. We also have the hybrids with the pure electric vehicles coming. Ultimately, we will have the hydrogen fuel cell and the cold fusion power plant. With the right "tranny," these fancy fuels can pull a load up a grade.

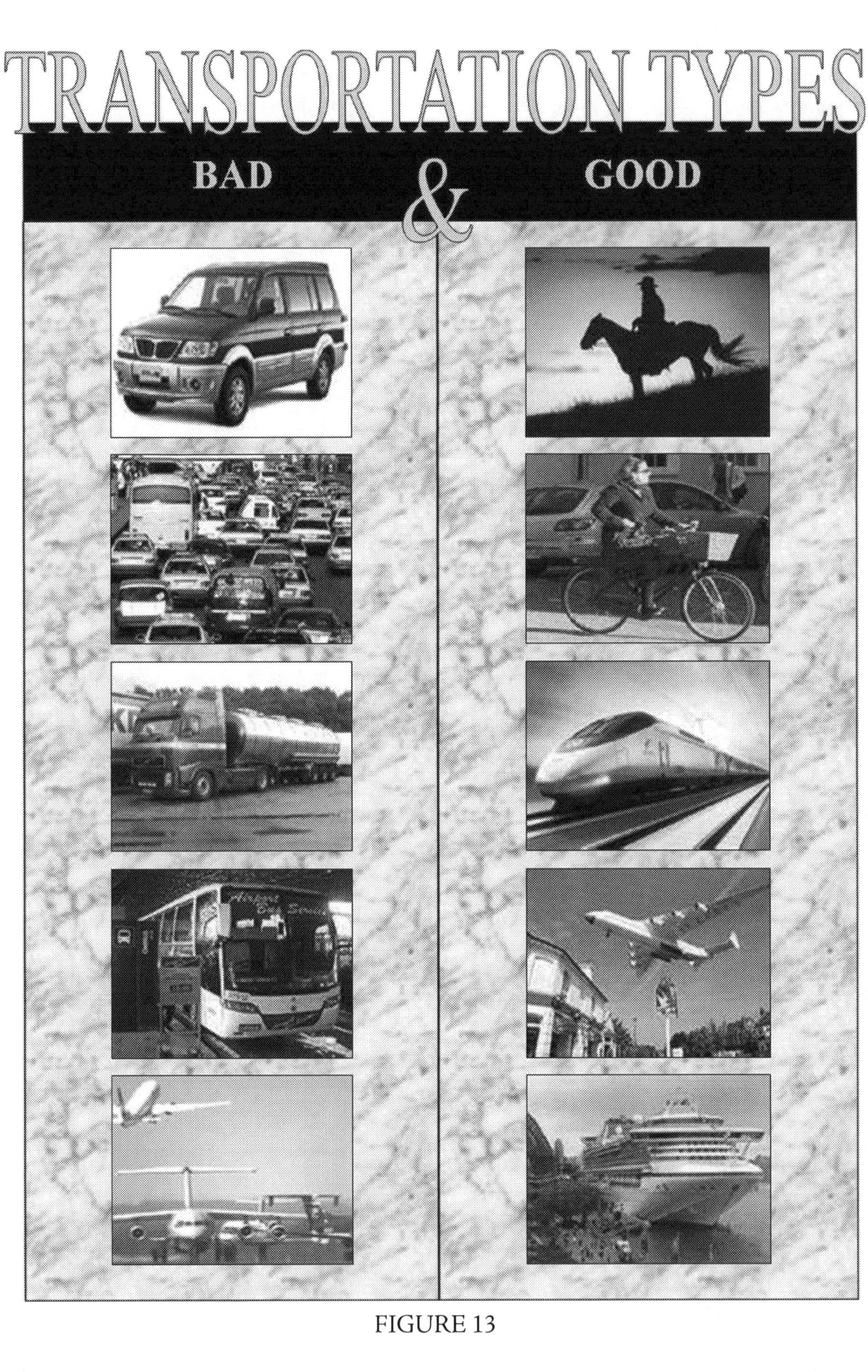

TRANSPORTATION TYPES

BAD & GOOD

FIGURE 13

58

All this adjustment would not be by government order, but by the libertarian law of supply and demand. Think of all the airliners that would no longer fill the air. Think of all the airport properties that don't have to be one fourth the size of the city they serve.

In the use of space and energy for non-polluting transportation and industry, emulate Europe. They know it can be done because they have done it. Eschew the way of India and China. They don't know it can be done because to try it would risk the stability of the state. At the requirements of environmental salvation, India and China balk like a frightened horse. Whenever the west challenges them to change, they point to our unwillingness to change. We must change and set them an ethical example.

HOMES AND AGRICULTURE

Both our homes and our agriculture have gone places and filled spaces they were not meant to.

In America and Canada, from a line through the west end of the Great Lakes to the Rocky Mountains and from Dallas, Texas to Edmonton, Alberta, Canada, the land is supposed to be the Great Plains. It is supposed to be grassland supporting large populations of herd animals – wild or domestic.

However, modern man has killed the wild animals and penned up the domestic animals. He has plowed up perhaps half of the plains for cash crop grains. According to the United States Department of Agriculture, the U.S. "heartland," plants 90 million acres of corn. In 2009, 65% of the corn went to cattle and pig feed lots as well as chicken and turkey farms. Then the penned up animals excrete dung that percolates methane into the air. 15% of greenhouse gases come from industrial animal husbandry.

In 2009, another 34% of the corn went to Ethanol. This corn biofuel costs as much as reformulated gasoline and gets about the same mileage. Ethanol's wonderful but only benefit is decreased emissions.

The remainder of the corn crop goes to high fructose corn syrup, corn starch, and corn oil. These are the starch "fillers" in processed foods. There is also some corn for corn meal and some canned and frozen corn…90 million acres for that…in the United States.

Then there's the wheat, barley, oats, and rye. These are grains for our high quality food. Well, a lot of the barley and rye goes to animals and horses get a jolt of oats now and again. Also, the refined white wheat flour is more starch that does us more harm than good. But when these grains are kept whole, they are our staff of life.

In the 1930's, the eastern portion of that former prairie that was plowed up for cash crop agriculture blew away in the "Dust Bowl." Now we have learned how to contour plow and do other things to hold the soil in place. Still, even without a dust bowl, global warming has produced chronic drought in the west. There is too much agriculture (or the wrong kind of agriculture) for the water available.

TOO MUCH AGRICULTURE

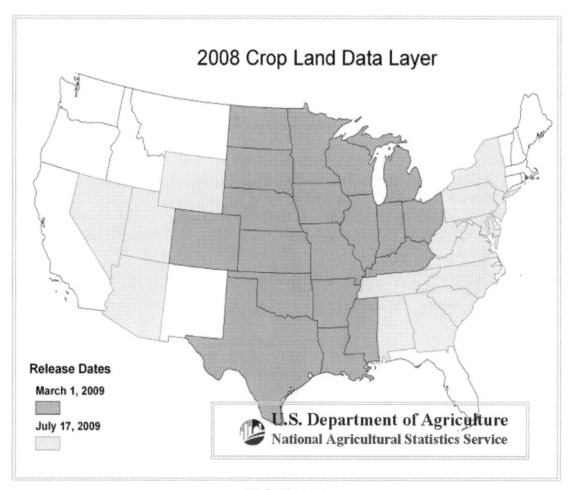

FIGURE 14

Tornado & Lightning

We have evolved a new weather pattern. Heat and dryness suck moisture out of the west and up into the higher atmosphere. This warm air is then drawn by prevailing winds eastward. The air mass becomes moist and precipitates rain or snow over the eastern United States. As the wind falls down along the precipitating cool or cold front, it recoils westward under the pressure of sea breezes bringing tropical storms up from the south Atlantic. This is a rolling circular air movement lying horizontally on the land. In the Midwest, if there is enough heat and humidity, such a horizontal air rotation would eventually get enough speed and momentum to rise up like a spinning top and become a tornado. Could this giant continental, horizontal, rolling, circular air movement stand up and become a continental tornado? This arrangement extends to the "prairie provinces" of Canada as well. (See National Geographic, February, 2008, "Drying of the West," Robert Kunzig.)

Global warming does not mean a simple, consistent movement to continual drought. The air is consistently ever warmer, but the moisture content of the atmosphere gyrates wildly. When winter finally comes to western North America, there may be light rain and snow with insufficient snowpack and emptying reservoirs or there may be continual rain and snow and monumental snowpack. In bad water years, the mountain forests and the high desert scrub become tinder dry and burst into cataclysmic wildfires. If a good water year follows a bad, the spring runoff hits the hillsides denuded of rooted foliage and there are mudslides to float Noah's ark. The classic example of this pattern is California, but the turbulence of drought and deluge is also upsetting Africa and China. (See *National Geographic*, July 2008, "Under Fire: Flames Threaten the American West Again," Neil Shea and *National Geographic*, April 2009, "Droughts and Deluges Could Stir Up Political unrest," Elizabeth Colbert)

Drought: Cracked Earth

Wildfire in Forest

Satellite View of Australia

As it is with North America, so it is with Australia. Called "the canary in the coal mine of global warming," Australia is in a state of permanent drought. The agriculture and population of Australia are in the southeast portion of the giant island continent. The crops in the cities are watered by the Murray River and the Darling River. Feeder streams come from the Australian Alps and the Great Dividing Range down into the Murray River and the Darling River. These great watercourses serve the Murray-Darling Basin. Now, despite dams and canal systems, the Murray and the Darling are drying up and all the agriculture and animal husbandry are going away.

Australians unwittingly added to their woes by trying for too much agriculture. They went northwest of the Darling River, even further "out back." They drilled wells in the desert and irrigated huge tracts. They doubled Australia's agricultural output.

Then an awesome thing happened. They drained the underground water table. They dragged what water was under the ground up to the surface, mixed with the salt in the soil. Now they have an endless landscape of salt rimed, poisoned sinkholes.

Adelaide, Australia sits at the mouth of the Murray and Darling Rivers where they empty into the Tasman Sea. Adelaide is the first city in the world to at least consider permanent water rationing. In one respect, the nation of Australia is now exactly like the nation of Saudi Arabia. Australia is now considering massive desalinization and purification of ocean water to satisfy the thirst of its land and its people. (See *National Geographic*, April 2009, "Australia's Dry Run: Farmers Feel Betrayed by the Climate," Robert Draper)

WHAT IS THE RIGHT USE OF SPACE?

Land: with a few famous exceptions in Japan and Arabia, they aren't making any more of it and the land we have is less and less useful because it is drier and drier.

Water: there is less of it in the places that need it most and too much in the places that have all they need. Less water in less land means less agriculture even though there are more people.

Air: it has too many hydrocarbons and not enough oxygen. It has too much smoke and not enough moisture. Air today is warm enough to melt the polar and Antarctic ice. This raises, chills and desalinates the oceans, which makes less land and destroys a system of ocean currents that have made habitable our northern lands. In many places, low air quality hurts animal (including human) life.

Farmed fish, cannibal turkeys, penned cows eating dried corn, pigs up to their bellies in their own dung: By land and by sea, we are hunting useful species to extinction and replacing them with animals of lesser value.

What is the right use of space? As with the right use of time, clarity comes from spirituality. God wants us to be in the right place at the right time. Because we have our free agency, we do not have to, but because we are spirit sons and daughters of Heavenly Father we ought to move forward through the eras and up to the highest level in all of our activities. We were told to "Be fruitful, and multiply, and replenish the earth, and subdue it: and have dominion over the fish of the sea, and over the fowl of the air, and over every living thing that moveth upon the earth." (Genesis 1:28) The case of Bishop Ussher reminded us that the Scriptures are as true as they are translated and interpreted correctly.

I say this means that people must be productive. We must have children, and multiply the human race, yes, but we must do so productively. We must build families that can create populations that will produce good and useful things to help the earth. *Pleno*, in Latin, is the verb "to fill." In Latin, *repleno* would be "refill." If we drain the water, foul the air, and consume the products of land and sea, then we are obligated to *refill* the earth... to give back what we took.

Because human beings are physical bodies inhabited by spirit sons and daughters of God or Heavenly Father, they are, therefore, a different order of being from the animals of the earth. They are not creatures of instinct, unless individuals choose to surrender to instinct (human nature). Otherwise, they are capable of controlling themselves and their environment more so than any other being on earth. Therefore, for better or for worse, they have dominion over the earth, which is, according to the dictionary, "the power or right of governing and controlling; sovereign authority. rule; control; domination."

Adam and Eve as metaphors for each and every one of us have been given the right to choose between everything we mean by God on the one hand and everything we mean by the devil on the other hand. We had the right to choose and also we were forced to choose between good and evil. We are free, which gives us authority or dominion over ourselves and our world. But the great moral law of freedom is that freedom isn't free. With every authority comes a responsibility. Thus, we have dominion over the world and we are responsible for the world. Our dominion is in reality a stewardship.

Remembering always that the spiritual life is a life of service, a life of thinking about other people, what, then, do we actually have to do with the world to cross over that critical line from mere humanity to a godlike spirituality?

First: we must pass out of the mineral era.

By this is meant that we must fully grasp what our minds have constructed with matter, energy, space, and time. We cannot be fixed on a mechanical "stone age."

➢ We must leave behind us forever the age of fossil fuel. We have gone beyond fire for energy. We cannot rape and flay the Earth for the energy that drives human society. We must transport ourselves and our goods in accordance with our most advanced and also our most ancient ideas about wind and water and sun in this mechanical, electromagnetic, and atomic universe.

➢ Also, we cannot hew building materials out of the living rock. We cannot build massive structures to house a few people. No more Stonehenge, no more pyramids, no more Parthenons, and no more capitols.

➢ We must place large communities in large structures. Think Manhattan rather than Los Angeles. Live in the air and the sun, supported by steel and surrounded by glass. The twin towers of the World Trade Center in New York were the right idea. They were brought down by anti-spiritual human conflict. Their replacement will be even stronger in the right direction.

➢ We must plan our communities. They must fit into the contour of the land.

➢ We have to spread out. We cannot cower in the good places, the easy places. We have to take back the desert and make it blossom as the rose. This means we have to make it rain. That brings us around to a connection with our requirement to leave behind us forever the age of fossil fuel, reducing greenhouse gases by 90%.

Second: we must leave behind us the era of plants.

By this is meant the era of plants as treasure, as a harvest of money more important than the natural world. We cannot be greedy and exploitative in our forestry, agriculture, and animal husbandry. It is bad to kill in order to build.

➢ Be very sparing in the use of trees. Build out of healthful synthetics that look like traditional materials. Forests make it rain. Forests cleanse the air. Build homes, towns, and roads among trees, not without trees. For every tree that makes way for a new structure, plant a new tree. Instruct every logger from the teak forests of Thailand to the spruce covered slopes of Oregon: you cut down a tree; you plant a tree.

Deforestation of Amazon

➤ Don't eradicate the rain forests to make money on cash crops. Harvest the miracle drugs, remedies, and nutraceutical foods that are provided by the rainforest. Ask any pharmaceutical giant. The real money is in healthcare.

➤ We cannot be greedy and exploitative in our agriculture. We must give the earth back to the oxygen creating, soil holding, water storing plants. When half of our crop goes to animal feed, and half of the rest goes to filler for junk food, because that is where agribusiness gets its profit, we are wrong. When we plow up land that is supposed to be grassy prairie, we invite the dust storm and the locust swarm and all the plagues of Egypt and the afflictions of Job. "I am the grass. Let me work," wrote Walt Whitman.

➤ Put the animals out on the grass where they belong. They will make better food and clothing because of it. Cities in the desert and farms in the river basin can only get as much water as the land can give. The really good things of the earth -- orchards, gardens, paddies, and wholesome whole grains for the human staff of life -- can be grown in a surprisingly small area. The 80% of our diet that should be fruits, vegetables, and whole grains can be grown on 20% of our land. This is particularly true when we bring the hydroponic garden inside with us, productive in winter and summer.

➤ Biofuels are good. Natural gas is better and fuel cells are better still, but biofuels are a good thing. However, don't devote 30,000,000 acres to corn for biofuel. Make some of the grass out there on the Prairie be switchgrass. World demand for processed, refined, white sugar is dropping, because simple carbohydrates are bad for people, but sugarcane and sugar beets make excellent biofuel (Cuba will be glad to know).

➤ It's okay to grow hay. Cured hay is the best animal feed out there.

➤ Solution to the tobacco problem: feed it green to the animals. Raw, green tobacco is extremely beneficial to animals. It is full of disease preventing, disease curing, and generally health promoting compounds. Consider it salad for cows. Outlaw the cured leaf and the inhalation of 4000 carcinogenic substances.

➤ Same deal for opium poppies, coca paste, and marijuana. Help Afghanistan, Colombia, and California go straight. Buy the crops legit. Extract the useful drugs and throw away the evil part. Cut out the middle drug lord.

➤ Put the animals out on the newly re-created range, and let them graze on the healthful grasses. The animals have their way of making the land fruitful and replenishing it.

Third: We have to leave behind the Animal Era.

Cow Grazing

By this is meant not that we have to eliminate all animals but rather that we have to cease eliminating all animals. By this is meant not that we cannot eat animals (although a healthy human should eat a diet that is 80% plants *as the plants came out of the ground*), but that we must make complete use of every part of every animal. Like our hunting ancestors, we respect animals. Leaving the Animal Era means acknowledging that we are more than just animals.

Grasslands must not be replaced by roads, buildings and the many things man needs to control his environment.

As man becomes more "civilized" he will find more efficient ways of getting his food, clothing and shelter and other necessities of life, than by the animal. Minerals are more plentiful and easier to use, once man has learned how. Today the natural homes of animals are being destroyed to make way for better homes for human beings. We must live in harmony with the animals. The metaphor of the zoo is good here. In an all natural, outdoor zoo (or "zoological garden"), the animal areas are carefully reconstructed natural habitat for each species of animal. The animals' way of life in their areas is much safer, less stressful, or more attractive than in the wild, although there are zoological parks where the animals are free on a small replica of their range and the humans pass through restricted to their vehicles.

Solar & Wind Farm

Solar power is the spiritual level of the ages of man. It will ultimately replace animal, human and fossil-fuel power. But until we get there, the world's muscle-psychology lingers on, even as the Automation and the Information Age take shape. Today man does not feel morally justified in taking a day's pay for anything but a day's muscle work. You can take the shovel out of the shoveler's hands, but you can't take the shovel-psychology out of the mind. Muscle thinking tends to keep people *muscle*-sized. In the Age of Aquarius to come, a higher "octave" of vibration and consciousness will develop. Then our love of the mind will rise above the current love of the physical body, and the physical body will tend to become smaller. (Or so it would seem.)

As I wrote in 1991,

Therefore, the next several hundred years, the average person will truly be a "stranger in paradise." Drastic steps will be needed to orient man properly to this higher level of living. Until this is done, it is likely that his subconscious mind, as well as his many misguided activities, will go right on creating the larger body of the caveman, instead of the smaller body of the more spiritual human being.

ON TO THE HUMAN ERA AS PREPARATION FOR THE SPIRITUAL

It's all biorelative. Spiritual living is an advanced art and philosophy that will have to be pursued with far greater skill and diligence than baseball or engineering. The spiritual inner life will require less muscle effort of the old type, of course, but many more times as much mental effort. There must be even more advanced muscle effort in the form of breathing exercises; also prayer, meditation, education, and the like, which one might refer to as biorelativity.

AUTOMATION.

Therefore, advanced automation will create unemployment and leisure for those who are *not ready* to live in the Spiritual Age, and for those who do not understand the new, higher level activities made possible by automation.

In the more distant future, people will tend to become more similar in physical size, color, and culture. Advanced science, automation, and freedom of movement in all parts of the planet evolve. Life the world over will tend to become more similar. Outward differences will tend to decrease, as they are already doing, and inward differences will tend to increase. Thought by thought more soul-awareness evolves . . . "and greater things than I do ye shall do." (John 14:12)

Yoga & Jog in Park

This slight decrease in man's physical size does not mean that man of the future will be a weakling. Man of the future will be able to run the *three* minute mile easier than man of today runs the four minute mile. A better more positive mind will create a better body, and will make it possible for people to do feats that are now called either impossible or "miracles." Sickness will become a thing of the past. The human being will achieve amazing feats with the subtle electromagnetic forces stored *in* the body. Spiritual living will be as unbelievable for the caveman of today as the computer age of today is unbelievable for the caveman of yesterday.

There is still another, and far more important aspect to man's decrease in physical size. Man of the future will learn to have much respect for the word relativity. For every step that man takes into the spiritual world, there will be a relative decrease in the relative importance of the physical body. Food and all of the necessities of life will be relatively easier to acquire. Some people on earth have already learned how to live without sickness, and without eating any liquids or solids. That certainly came as a BIG surprise to me. I honestly did not think it was possible.

Jesus said, "Man does not live by bread alone." (Matt 4:4, Deut 8:3) By this he meant, of course, that people are not happy with physical gratification alone. In the literal case of food, we are trying to undo bad "programming" and redo good "programming." We are trying to leave behind the fear of starvation out on the veld. We are trying not to gorge on the good kill. Spiritual people know about the *health* benefits of fasting and caloric restriction.

Really the only unnatural eaters in the world are the Americans. Everybody else eats natural food in a natural way and they are smaller and their food is grown in a smaller area. They have fewer animals that, naturally, eat less. Their animals eat their natural food. They don't eat processed animal food any more than those people eat processed food. Thus, their food is grown in a more natural way in a better use of agricultural land.

This will save a great amount of wear and tear on the physical body. Gradually, man will evolve into something which is more than a man, even as man of today has already evolved into something which is more than an animal. If man never changed his way of life, he would never become anything but a man. However, in this DYNAMIC world, neither man nor any creature in all creation can remain the same. All things are evolving upward and must continue.

Today there are many times more people living in just one city than lived in all of America in 1600. Thus, as the population increased some 250 times in about 400 years, the average creative ability of people increased thousands, millions and even billions of times. That is *dynamic*.

Man's physical body became *relatively* smaller; man's mental body became relatively larger. The use of a higher level of intelligence caused a higher level of consciousness to evolve.

The present scare about the "population explosion" is an outstanding example of our caveman type of thinking. The human being is looked upon with a negative frame of reference. More is thought to be worse. That is partly due to the fact that the Age of Pisces is to the solar cycle what January is to the earth's cycle, so to speak. This is a kind of spiritual ice age. In these times nearly all societies of humans speak about overpopulation, because people are so often caught in the chilly grip of this spiritual ice age. Transportation has been poor and so the people remained isolated, in places like Africa. When you can't find the God within, you are sure to turn to the five senses without. That causes overpopulation.

TO LIVE AND DIE IN THE COUNTRY

In the austere environments of the primitive and the developing world, such as western China, Siberia, South Asia, Africa, Latin America … oh, wait … *everywhere in the world except for Europe, Britain, and America*, people who have evolved in a rural wilderness environment for thousands of years don't want to do it anymore. Because of climate change, desertification, crumbling of political and social order, disillusion with the tribal way of life, and the enticements of modern technological life, nobody wants to live in the country anymore, because the country is uninhabitable.

Everywhere except in the developed west, people are migrating to cities. *The Christian Science Monitor* of January 12, 2007 reported the United Nations saying that, in 2008, for the first time in human history, more than half the world's population lived in cities. There are twenty-two megacities in the world with over ten million people some of which are mega mega cities with over twenty million people. In the city there is life. There is work. There is opportunity. There is security. There is no culture or spirit but what people bring with them from their "home," but that is all right. Culture and spirit don't take up much *space*.

Where does the food come from? In America, we cover millions of acres with crop land, but that is to produce millions of bushels of grain to feed millions of animals. Also, there is a lot of junk grain to make junk food for obese people who shouldn't be eating that stuff. But 80% of the fruits and vegetables eaten by all of America are raised in southern California. California and Florida have lost a lot of their citrus groves but Arizona has taken up the slack. Florida has far more cattle than Texas taking up far less space. The Mekong Delta in little Vietnam raises three bumper crops of rice every year, exporting rice to all of Asia (and America). In or near every megacity in the world are huge "truck gardens" supplying huge "farmers markets." In the cities themselves, all those displaced "internal immigrant" country people raise food in hydroponic, rooftop, window box, and back yard gardens, chicken coops, duck ponds, and pig sties.

Rural & City Poverty

Life is terrible and people are starving *out in the country*. In the city, life is terrible in the horrible slums when you first get there but then you can make a life. You can rule over your little space.

In the developed world, the people have the option of land intensive agriculture and they take it. Country people can be *very* successful if they turn over their family farms to agribusiness and become agricultural workers.

Aerial Suburbs

Meanwhile, the highest level people are a new upper middle class that may have been raised in the country but now has to work in the city. These people owe their success to their work in the city but they cannot stand to live in the city. They have created a new space wasting environment called *suburbs*. Suburbs require lots of everything bad and sprawl over everything good. Urban and suburban sprawl is a "traffic jam" of hastily built structures. It looks like overpopulation, but as with the freeway rush hour traffic jam, it is just a waste of space.

THE CITY WITHIN A BUILDING

A TALE OF TWO CITIES

New York puts seven million people in 368 square miles. It is surrounded by a metropolitan area (suburbs) with eighteen million people in 1,148 square miles. Los Angeles puts seven million people in 4,850 square miles. It is surrounded by a metropolitan area (suburbs) with twelve million people in around 30,000 (inhabited) square miles.

In the 2000 census, there were twenty-three million motor vehicles registered in Los Angeles County. That same year there were eleven million vehicles registered in the New York metropolitan area.

Aerial Manhattan

There has been public transportation in New York for at least 150 years. There have been subways serving all parts of New York City for one hundred years. There has been public transportation in Los Angeles for eighty-five years and light rail (elevated and subway) for ten years. Commuter rail has moved an average of four million people a day into and out of New York City since 1958. Commuter rail in New York began in 1920. There is no commuter rail in Los Angeles.

The pattern is clear. New York is a vertical city where people move about on public transportation. Los Angeles is a horizontal city where people move about in private vehicles.

There are cities like New York and cities like Los Angeles all over the world.

We are striving to cross over some critical line between an over sophisticated human level existence to a holistic, wise, ecologically sound existence that encourages a spiritual way of life.

Aerial Los Angeles

The high rise city develops high consciousness people.

Imagine large numbers of people living in a nourishing, relaxing, comfortable amount of space, not crammed, not jammed, in the midst of a three dimensional city made not of mineral level huge stone blocks, but of metal, glass, and composite materials. People are living in the sky, connected, familial, collegial, even tribal, but not impersonal. Each family owns its own wonderfully sufficient space.

I am describing a 21st century "development" in housing that is the mixed use, urban village. This is a vertical, almost cubic, relatively small footprint village in the center of the city. It is condominium apartments, rented apartments, shopping including supermarkets, health spa, professional services including clinics, office buildings, movie theaters, live theaters, concert halls, museums, park, pre-school/daycare, hotel, police station, convention center, and television/radio station, all connected by gorgeously landscaped walkways, people movers, escalators, and elevators. People that live here do have cars. They are in the underground parking. They are in use maybe once a week when somebody wants to leave the city completely. There is no need to drive around the city. You can go from your city in a building in the sky to another city in a building in the sky on silent, elegant, public transportation.

Here's the thing. Living in a city in a building in the sky demands that you are progressing from an advanced human to a spiritual way of life. Animal level behavior is intolerable in a city in a building in the sky. The city in a building in the sky encloses life. It encloses good life. It encloses bad life. The closer people are to you, the more they affect you. You must eschew low level people. Get away from the lower levels in everything. Seek out the high levels.

Also, we can spread out if we do it in the right way, taking back the grasslands and the wetlands and the woodlands from the desert and the strip mines and the ocean storm surge, but we spread out into networks of homes, villages, towns, and cities that are connected to the support of the wider world by electronics and intermodal high speed transportation which ends with a biohummer from the station to the house. That is community in a spiritual age.

CHAPTER SIX

CONFLICT BETWEEN CREATION AND CONSUMPTION; IT MAKES COMPLEXITY.

COMPLEXITY OF CREATION

A pile of minerals is capable of little more than chemical action, in and of itself. Plants are higher in level of consciousness and can use the process of photosynthesis for growth. Animals are higher than plants in consciousness. They can move about and care for their young. Some can build homes and lay up scarce foods for the future. They can also show much love and affection for their own species, as well as use other species for food. There are animals that can relate personally to humans as domestic animals. These simple statements hint at the complexity of creation.

The real complexity comes from the ability of the thinking human to perceive complexity and indeed add to complexity. This can be good or bad as the human thinks carnally or naturally or, on the other hand, thinks spiritually. Spiritual thinking becomes instrumental in the processes which lead to *soul-awareness* within. I call this creating since the soul is a specialized unit of God. The soul knows what God knows because it has omnipresence with God. Separateness is man's illusion. God is all in All. Therefore, the spiritual soul is a Creator, and man can create once soul-awareness has been achieved.

The processes of creation encompass all other processes of being. There is a degree of creation in every movement of everything. There are levels of creation. The highest level is that which uses the least amount of consumption of existing materials in the making or creating of the greatest amount of new materials. When things are made as if by no practical means or by "miracle," one is dealing with the highest human technology or the critical line just beyond which is the spiritual level of creation and complexity.

The higher the level of complexity, the higher will be the level of the human being. Each level is more complex than the level below or before it. The mineral level is the least complex. The spiritual level is the most complex.

The mineral is the lowest level of being; therefore, it is logical that man has made some of his greatest achievements in the mineral sciences. Nuclear energy is one of the greatest discoveries.

The saddest thing about the mineral level of progress is the fact that these discoveries cannot be controlled for positive purposes since man's spiritual level of science is the least developed. Thus it is so likely that nuclear energy will be used to hurt instead of help. Loving thy neighbor as thyself is not too easy to learn during the present "spiritual ice age." Today we can use the five senses the best. The sixth sense is not so easy when both you and your neighbor are competing for the same barrel of scarce oil.

Man's knowledge is small because he has just begun to study. It was only 1945 when man discovered how to utilize atomic energy effectively. If man has just learned about the atomic realm of minerals, the least complex of creation, is it not true that his knowledge of higher things is still more remote?

In the future, man's knowledge will grow by leaps and bounds. The discovery of atomic energy at the mineral level will unlock many closed doors at every higher level of complexity. Today man depends largely upon plants and animals for food. Tomorrow he will do more to tap the endless supply of the mineral level of foods, including the subtle life-force type, also called cosmic energy or the WORD, of which all minerals are made. Once man has freed himself from the slavery of food-getting, or "earning his living by the sweat of his brow," he will be able to devote more and more of his time to the higher levels of complexity, including the spiritual or the *superconscious soul* within.

Learning the way will be man's major problem and task in the future. Christ said, "I am the way, the truth and the life," (St. John 14:6). Conquest of the spiritual level of complexity, or science, will require all of man's time and all of his powers. In that sense, there can be no "leisure" time for man of the future. Leisure time, like unemployment, hunger, overpopulation, war, sickness and the like, are all things of primitive man. The more civilized or conscious man becomes, the less he will be concerned with such negative ideas. The more one learns, the more there is to learn in this DYNAMIC world. The more one discovers, the more there is to discover, until one becomes *soul aware*.

CREATION AND CONSUMPTION IN CONFLICT

Mankind today is still struggling under the negative weight of past dogmas and fixations. It was a mere 500 years since Columbus proved the earth was round. Therefore, in spite of rockets which can go to the moon, we are still struggling from the fixations formed during the Isolation Age. Race hates race. Nation hates nation. Religion hates religion. Labor hates management. West hates East. Continent hates continent. Young hate old. Public hates private. Poor hate rich. Party hates party. In fact, nearly all of man's social structure is honeycombed with negative thinking and stressful living. Thus some 80 to 90% of all illnesses are caused by stress or psychosomatic problems.

Here are a few specific examples of these areas of negativity.

➢ Transportation: Some 180 million vehicles kill about 50,000 American people per year, with about 1,000,000 wounded. Think of the grief caused to so many people. Nearly half of those killed are killed by drunk drivers.

➢ American drivers consume about 2.7 billion gallons of beer and 240 million gallons of liquor. What a nightmare of traffic to endure each day! Then add 23 million on illegal drugs.

➢ How can education survive under such stress?

➢ All of five years in World War II only killed 400,000 people for America.

➢ This stressful living kills about 500,000 Americans per year from heart-ailments alone.

> Fire: The problem of fire, as a means of energy release, is reaching catastrophic portions. The earth's 400 million motor vehicles put out some 8 billion tons of carbons yearly.

> Government spending (and debt) to prevent, deal with, and recover from catastrophic aggression and crime.

> National debt begins to strangle the entire nation. Global debt strangles the world.

> Debts are so high there is little money for education. And the money we needed to harness clean solar energy was wasted on polluting energy release. We have multi trillion dollar cleanup dilemma.

> All of this wasteful living has driven people out of schools and into drugs, other addictions, and a life of crime. Thus, health, wealth and willpower are depleted.

Millions are hungry and undernourished. Some 23 million are on illegal drugs. Millions are poorly housed. Millions live in varying degrees of slavery. Millions work in filthy and contaminated conditions not fit for animals. Millions die in accidents and wars. Millions have mental disorders. And *still* the world lives in fear of nuclear holocaust from resurgent superpower-ism as well as from the new "rogue states."

Whole civilizations direct their major efforts of life toward either the goals of conquest and aggression, or the opposition to aggression, which is almost as negative.

The weight of these burdens of negation has almost driven man to the wall. People spend about as much money on devices to keep themselves unconscious as they do for means to raise consciousness through education. We spend billions of dollars on drugs, alcohol, tobacco, gambling, and other devices to deaden the sensibilities to the negation of this age. This is not godly. This is not human. We may have the possibility of rising to the next level, but not the opportunity. Many have about as much morality as a rock and not much more love than a plant or animal in this period of global madness.

The formation of sovereign nations on planet earth was a very necessary step in cultural evolution. Sovereignty gave people security for growth in unstable surroundings. But once that growth has been made, and technology has advanced, those same sovereign borders which once gave protection, now give isolation and prevent further growth.

Immigration, or should we say, migration is key to the great transition from a lower to a higher level of consciousness, humanity, and spirituality if it is from destroyed wilderness to well planned city, from dark land ruled by wickedness to land of light with hope for all, or from poor land without educational or economic opportunity to a great souled and big hearted society.

When America was "empty" and a "new world," America was the paradigm for immigration solving world problems. This charity was a good deal. We got the best of the dissatisfied refugees (Remember Einstein?).

The problem comes when the entire population of a devastated land wants to move in a body to a new land. Now we have population shift to go along with climate shift and pole shift. The paradigm here is the decline and fall of the Roman Empire. In the fourth century, "barbarians" on the German border with Roman Gaul were being pushed into the Empire by migrations behind them. Barbarian, by the way, is the Latin word for foreigner. These foreign new-comers promised to live as good citizens of the empire and even to serve in imperial forces guarding the border they had just crossed. But when the entire population of "Germania" came over, they utterly disrupted Gallo-Roman life and ended up taking over everything and destroying the civilization created by Rome.

The nation state is not dead yet. Globalism and global village are good, but they require global law and global spirituality. The humane management of mass migration as a feature of development and not of decay is a sign of the times. It requires a high degree of the consciousness, high human level development and desire for spirituality for which we are striving.

Thus positive people use complexity and, indeed, perplexity, as an opportunity to resolve conflict to encourage advancement in this dynamic world.

AREAS of CREATION & CONSUMPTION

CREATION	CONSUMPTION
1. Education	1. Energy Release
2. Government	2. Food
3. Occupation	3. Transportation
4. Population	
5. Religion	
6. Communication	

LEVELS OF COMPLEXITY OF CREATION

LEVELS	COMPLEXITY
Spiritual	Creating
Human	Thinking
←————— CRITICAL LINE —————→	
Animal	Survival Skills
Plant	Growing, Producing
Mineral	

LEVELS OF SCIENCE (KNOWLEDGE)

LEVELS	SCIENCE
Spiritual	Religion, Philosophy
Human	Physics, Communication
←————— CRITICAL LINE —————→	
Animal	Zoology, Animal Husbandry
Plant	Botany, Agriculture
Mineral	Chemistry, Building

FIGURE 15

Now we have a good grounding in what I am setting forth as my premises and my testimony of life and the future. You see the great transitional moment in time and space to which our creation and evolution has brought us.

Now let us examine how we got to this point. How did the plan of salvation unfold on our earth through the eras, levels, and activities of we who are all children of God?

CHAPTER SEVEN
Dynamic ERAS of CREATION

The creation of the earth covered at least three to five billion years. During those billions of years continuous change took place. In what we refer to as the beginning, the earth started as a huge, unruly mass of hot, swirling, gaseous material. One or more billions of years passed before it had cooled and consolidated enough to allow any form of life to evolve.

At first there was mostly chemical change. Later, the materials became half chemical, half organic. One-celled plants and animals began to appear. Water and air evolved. Mountains and oceans came into being. Each change in the environment brought about a corresponding change in the plants and animals which were forced to adapt themselves to these changes. Those that made the best adaptations lived. Those that failed became extinct. There were also those that adapted themselves so well and became so fixed that when the next change came, they too, became extinct. Man is a creature which can adapt itself well and yet not become too fixed so that further changes cannot be made.

NAMES AND CHARACTERISTICS OF ERAS

These materials were taken from *The World Book Encyclopedia* 1958, Vol. 7, pp. 2924-2925, published by Field Enterprises Educational Corporation, Chicago.

ARCHEOZOIC. The archeozoic era was the first era. The name comes from the Greek word *archaios* which means "ancient." It also means "beginning" or "course" or "beginning of a course" as in arc or arch or archery. The *zoic* part of each word comes from another Greek word *zoe* which means "life." The act of creation during the Archeozoic Era was the formation of various minerals. Toward the end of this era, it is possible that simple one-celled plants and animals evolved from the half-mineral, half-organic chemicals of the time. Thus Ancient life, as the name suggests, did exist on earth after the first several billion years of this era.

The Archeozoic Period or Eon or Era is also known as the *Pre-Cambrian Era* or "Time of Beginnings" ("In the beginning…?"). This is the time of the formation of the Earth's crust, evolving into the earth's surface with the first primitive bacteria in its soil.
(1 to 3 billion B.C.)
Limy sea plants continued to build rocks.
Limy sea plants built deposits of rocks in East Canada and West.
No fossils known (2.1 to 3 billion B.C.).

PROTEROZOIC. The Proterozoic Era is the second era of creation. The Greek word *protos* means first. First forms of life began to appear above the one-celled type of plant and animal. However, the main activity of the era was still that of the mineral level of the first era.

(490 million to 1 billion B.C.)

Shelled animals in sea; stony plants were abundant.

PALEOZOIC. The Paleozoic Era was the third era. Its name comes from the Greek word *palios* which means "ancient" or "old." During this era the most outstanding development was the huge plant growth. For example, the plants of the Carboniferous Period, which resulted in much of our present day supply of coal, oil, and natural gas were grown in the Paleozoic Era.

(190 to 490 million B.C.)
1. Carboniferous period (220 to 280 mil. B.C.) trees,
    ferns, vines, bushes in swamps.
2. Devonian period—first trees grew in swamps; coral and sea animals.
3. Silurian period—land plants appeared; many shelled animals in sea.

MESOZOIC. The Mesozoic Era was the fourth era. The name comes from the Greek word *mesos* meaning middle. It is sometimes called the "Age of Reptiles," due to the huge size and number of reptiles then.

(60 million B.C. to 190 million B.C.)

Huge dinosaurs in western swamps (115-155 million B.C.)

CENOZOIC. The Cenozoic Era is the fifth era (Sixth if we start with the creation of the universe). The name comes from the Greek word *kainos*, which means "recent" or new." This era is also called the "Age of Mammals," because so many giant mammals ruled the major part of the land at that time. During the last few million years, the mammal man made his appearance on planet Earth.

(11,000 B.C. to 60 million B.C.)

1. Human beings reached Europe (2 million B.C.)
2. Last dinosaurs died out (by 60 million B.C.)

Conclusions about the five geologic eras of creation:

1. Minerals are generally formed first, about 3 to five billion years ago.

2. The carboniferous period, during which plants were grown to produce coal, came after (that is, since) 3 billion B.C.

3. The Age of Reptiles, during which dinosaurs were so plentiful, came after the carboniferous period.

4. Man only came onto the scene during the last few million years and …

5. Something scientists cannot perceive and something religionists cannot fail to perceive happened no later than 6,000 years ago to make modern man something separate from Cro-Magnons, Neanderthals, and "homo sapiens" generally.

Let us find the trends in these five geological eras and see what Trend of All Trends appears from them.

The dominant trend that emerges from a chronological ordering of these eras is that creation of the Earth proceeds from minerals to plants to animals to humans.

If we claim that God did put into a human being one of his spirit sons (the "Adam and Eve effect") and thus launch *conscious* humanity, then the word *spiritual* will be used to describe any kind of creation in the Cenozoic Era beyond (or, in chart form, above) the human level.

When God "breathed the breath of life" into Adam – that is, "inspired" him or "put a spirit in" him, the trend of the eras of creation went over a *Critical Line* into the highest level within the Cenozoic Era which pointed toward a materialistic development of human society so great that it would have the capability of destroying both society and the planetary environment that had given it birth. Maybe this is what the Tower of Babel means to us today. We have built our tower as high as we can and now it will fall down. The old 1931 Harburg and Gorney song says,

> Once I built a tower
> Way up to the sun
> Of bricks and mortar and lime.
> Once I built a tower
> And now it's done.
> Buddy, can you spare a dime.

This is the theoretical (and foretold) outcome of three to five billion years of creation. The six eras or stages or periods (metaphorical "days") of creation having evolved, the spiritual level is in the process of being created. The spiritual level has not become a predominant reality for mankind. In fact, human society is developing along two tracks which are in – I would say – an unnecessary conflict. These are secular humanism and spirituality or, as it is often put, science and religion.

There is an old saying in business. "Spreadsheets do not lie." When we put these huge concepts into a simple chart, we see we are approaching an end and a beginning, a transformation. We can use the secular humanist science to predict climatic destruction and social suicide through conflict over the scraps of planetary resources that remain. Alternately, we can use the spiritual, religious approach of heeding psychic, spiritual prophets, ancient and modern, We are then able to face the end of things as they are and the change into things as they will be.

Combining true science and true religion, we see that the mathematical and spiritual prophecies say what must be if we choose wrong and what may be if we choose right. Using thus proven science and thus proven religion, let us advance through the destructive end of the cycle of creation into *The Spiritual Age of the future*.

Some might notice that the trend of all trends in Figure 1 is little more than basic evolution. This is not entirely true. It is the purpose of the method of this book to take the known part of the universe and to try to identify trends which will make the unknown a little less unknown. The top and the bottom of each trend are usually in the realm of the unknown, while the trend suggested by the more familiar middle levels sheds some light upon both of the unknown ends.

FINDING MEANING IN THE TREND OF THE ERAS

The spiritual level of development is the last sliver of the Cenozoic Era, so small that it cannot be given as a major characteristic of the era. Man is still too much of a man to be called a spiritual being until the end of the era. However, mankind quests for the spiritual level of being throughout the era.

An inspection of the progress of the eras reveals a paradox. When we look back at the Chart of Creation and Consumption (Figure 15 on Page 75), we see that human civilization consumes "down" through the eras in order to create "up" toward the spirituality toward which the Cenozoic Era is heading. That is to say, man consumes animal and plant life to nourish, clothe, and house himself. This enables him to fabricate vehicles and structures of all kinds out of minerals and fuel them with fossil remains of plants that may be in mineral form. With this fabric of civilization, man can research and learn about the structures and systems of the universe and engage in the most advanced thinking and observations leading back "up" to entry into spiritual realms.

The general trend in evolution is the important thing to consider, not the specific details. In broad terms, the Age of the Animal definitely came after the Age of the Plant. One great proof of this is the fact that geologists discovered that the Age of Reptiles came in the Mesozoic Era, millions of years after the age when giant plant formations prepared the materials for petroleum and coal formations during the carboniferous period of the Paleozoic Era. The time periods of these major events starts to shape the time trend.

Then, during this most recent part of the Cenozoic Era, spiritual events moved us toward a spiritual age or era. The birth of Jesus is acknowledged by much of the world's population as an outstanding example of a spiritual event. We see this in the marking of time as "before Christ" (B.C.) and "in the year of the Lord" (A.D. Anno Domini). Even people uncomfortable with acknowledging the existence of Christ as opposed to just Jesus still are bound to say "before the common era" (B.C.E.) and "(in) the common era" (C.E).

These five eras tend to document the trend of time of creation. The trends in size and complexity also support this trend of time. As time went by, the evolutionary environment of planet earth continually improved and the things which evolved as a result of this improvement also continually improved and resulted in higher levels of being.

In assessing the trend of planetary creative time periods, we must accept the possibility of conditions on a planet which would produce variations to the trend. But it seems that after perhaps fifteen billion years, a system of suns and planets has evolved within galaxies of about 100 billion suns each. After billions of more years, planets have formed and cooled enough to solidify into minerals, then evolve the conditions and materials of life, then form plants, then animals, then humans and finally, spiritual beings.

It also seems possible that there are some planets which might never evolve conditions which will support plants, animals and human beings; not even until the solar system arrives at the supernova stage, some five billion years in the future. But regardless of what situation exists on a given planet, the trend of evolution for all the humanly habitable planets of the universe is generally: from mineral to plant, to animal, to human, to spiritual.

This theory assumes that all suns are composed of about the same thing, about 75% hydrogen. Also, they operate in about the same way. It further assumes that all galaxies are about the same, each evolving from lower to higher levels of being.

The past three to five billion years have been years of natural evolutionary growth for planet earth. Whenever natural growth takes place on any evolving planet, with about the same basic relationships to its solar system as those of the earth to its solar system, the level of life on that planet will achieve a state of dominance in much the same order as mineral, plant, animal, human and spiritual. This is the theory supporting the trend of the eras.

Now we must examine *levels* of creation through the eras to see the increasing value of each level. By catching this vision of the increasing worth of the levels over the time of the eras, we see the trend of where we are going and we see the good that our goal does for us.

CHAPTER EIGHT
Dynamic LEVELS of Being

We have seen that there were five dynamic eras of creation in the history of the earth. Before these five dynamic eras, there was an enormous piece of the fabric of time devoted to the creation and evolution of the universe of which our earth is an infinitesimally small part.

We have reasoned statistically that there must be a multitude of planets like ours in this enormous unfolding of the universe. We have decided that the creation and evolution of the universe, along with the five dynamic eras of creation of our earth, make the six creative periods or "days" spoken of in Scripture. We are further decided that the seventh "day," the day of rest, was a time when human beings or modern man or Homo sapiens evolved from primates. Finally, we decide to conclude that God, Heavenly Father, the Master of the Universe created our world (or, for those committed to Christianity absolutely, delegated to his Son the mission of creating, ruling over, and saving our world).

There is only one way to account for the break between naturally evolving humans to a mankind that is so conscious that people can build what they imagine even when what they imagine has no "physical" existence. This is our conclusion that, when the six creative periods and the rest period were over, Heavenly father "transplanted" one of his spirit sons and one of his spirit daughters into the human bodies of the literal or (if you think so) metaphorical, Adam and Eve.

At this point, we are in the human time near the end of the Cenozoic Era. Cultures and religions all around the world, ancient and modern, agree that we are approaching the end of the last era. Now we, the spirit sons and daughters of God, embodied in the human race, are free to choose to advance into a spiritual age.

The end of the world as we know it will come only when all of the signs of the times prophesied have come to pass. No matter whether this includes stars lining up, our sun being positioned properly in its astral cycle, the climax of climate devastation on the earth, human wickedness reaching an unbearable level, or all of these things, we are commanded to use our agency to save the world as best we can. By doing the will of God in this manner, we influence the millennial era, be it the second coming of the Savior or any other world climax. With righteousness, we defer the end of the world. We actually facilitate its transformation to the Kingdom of Heaven. God commands us to do that.

We want to be more spiritual and we're trying to learn how. Understanding the Dynamic Eras of Creation helps us. Now we will understand more when we see the level of creation in each of the Eras.

➤ The time of the creation of the universe and the Archeozoic Era of the creation of this earth are times of *mineral creation*. This *mineral level* of creation is the first level in time and in worth or value. It is the foundation level, making possible all other levels. It is the crudest, simplest level.

➢ The Proterozoic Era continues the mineral level and shows the beginning of both the *plant* and the *animal levels*. In this era, shelled animals live in the sea and stony plants – like coral -- are abundant. The simplest one-celled plants and animals are a much higher level of creation than the most complex of rocks and ores. The planet now hosts life with its inhalation and its exhalation, its ingestion, digestion, and excretion, its reproduction, growth, and death. The intelligence in the universe is now apparent in the genetic coding and the DNA of life. Behavior, however instinctual, makes these creatures living, independent beings. This is an infinitely higher level of creation than the mineral.

➢ The Paleozoic Era completes the evolution from the mineral level of creation to the *plant level of creation*. Now there is soil… land. There are trees and swamps, ferns and vines, grasses and bushes… vegetation of all kinds. Now plants rule the earth. Their ingestion of carbon dioxide and their exhalation of oxygen create an atmosphere for life. Out of the Paleozoic era comes the carboniferous era. Vast reaches of thick vegetation are overlain with more minerals. Those underground repositories of decaying vegetation become reservoirs of petroleum and veins of coal. Animals have evolved to quite complex shellfish and other sea creatures seen in fossils today.

➢ In the Mesozoic Era, animals come ashore. First, there are amphibians. Then there are land lizards. These evolve to our familiar dinosaurs. Mammals and birds develop. . Now there are parents and young. Now there are kinship groups, herds, burrows, and nests. Now there is hunting and gathering, predators and prey, communication and decision. There is territory. There is family. There is home. This is the *animal level of creation*, infinitely higher than the plant level.

➢ Lastly, there is the Cenozoic Era. The dinosaurs die and the mammals rule. There are birds, insects, reptiles, and mammals large and small -- creatures of the land, sea, and air. Then the primates arrive. Some of them become hominids. Some hominids become Cro-Magnons. Some Cro-Magnons become Neanderthals. This is caveman. In some way, either through the Cro-Magnons and then the Neanderthals or in addition to that progression, modern man arrives with tribes and fire and tools and weapons and language and art and structures and religion. These people endure climate change to include an ice age. This is the human being. This is Wise Man –Homo sapiens. *But* this is not a child of God. These are not spirit sons and daughters of God, which spirit children were transplanted from the Kingdom of God or God's world somewhere out there on the astral plane to inhabit and animate the mortal bodies of human beings. That was Adam and Eve. Adam and Eve kicked off the Plan of Salvation. This is the *Human Era* within the Cenozoic Era. The Cenozoic Era gives us the *human level of creation*.

➢ At the end of the Cenozoic Era, humanity is so greatly developed, so highly evolved, and with such enormous capabilities that it must either expend its energy on ultimate consumption and selfish satisfaction or reach within to attain a *spiritual level* of power and achievement. Because, in the Cenozoic Era, human beings from Adam and Eve forward are spirit sons and daughters of Heavenly Father and Heavenly Mother clothed in mortal bodies, they have free agency. Each human individual can choose what he or she will do with his or her development, evolution, and capability. Thus, each human individual is responsible for his or her progression to the spiritual level, which is the highest level in the last era of life on Earth.

So, the Five Dynamic Eras of Creation or Being give rise to the Five Dynamic Levels of Creation or Being. Those levels are the mineral, plant, animal, human and spiritual. These are literally levels of complexity and capability in the evolution of the Earth. They are also metaphorical levels of value in the progression of the earth through the Plan of Salvation.

These are the things of which man is made. These are the things all around man, which help or hurt him according to the laws of creation. These are the things which man must understand better and use more wisely. These five levels of being applied to the five eras of being are seen at work in the in the *Five Dynamic Activities of Creation or Being*.

5 DYNAMIC LEVELS OF CREATION

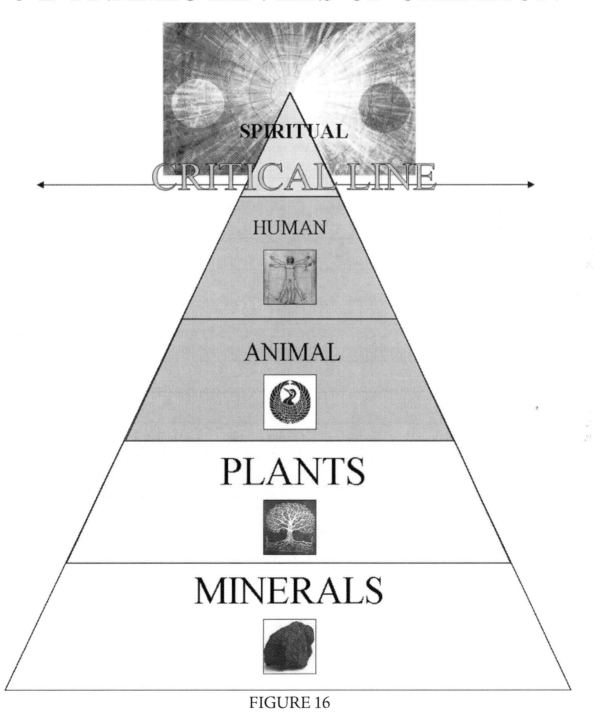

FIGURE 16

CHAPTER NINE
DYNAMIC ACTIVITIES OF CREATION

In Chapter Seven, the Five Dynamic Eras of Being for the Earth were considered. In Chapter Eight, the Five Dynamic Levels of Being were shown as a direct result of the five eras.

Chapter Nine will now center its attention upon the fourth level of creation, the *human*. All human activity is divided into *Five Dynamic Activities of Creation*. The five major activities or areas are

- ➢ *education,*
- ➢ *government,*
- ➢ *occupations,*
- ➢ *communication, and*
- ➢ *religion.*

Since our goal is the attainment of the Spiritual Level in all of our activities, we will evaluate these human activities using the qualitative metaphor of the Levels of Creation.

- ➢ We remember that the mineral level is chronologically and metaphorically the lowest level of complexity and utility.
- ➢ Next in time, complexity, and utility -- both literally and metaphorically –is the plant level.
- ➢ Then we rise to the animal level.
- ➢ Finally we attain the human level.
- ➢ Lastly, we may choose to do what is necessary to pass on to the spiritual level.

Thus we move from consumption to creativity.

The term creation, as it is used here, also includes the concept of consumption. The two happen simultaneously. Consumption is often called death. Death is another one of those relative terms in the language of any people which is confusing and actually impossible to describe well. For a thing like death does not really exist and, therefore, cannot be described. A better word for both the processes of consumption and creation is *change*. Each change each second, is the "death" or end of one thing and the "birth" or beginning of another thing. Thus the word death is very much the same as the word consumption and the word birth is much like the word creation. Both terms actually mean life, but from different frames of reference.

To evaluate the quality of our activities in order to morally and ethically decide what we ought to do, we have to add to our system of eras and levels one more scale of judgment.

As Figure 17 shows, we describe our human activities using a scale from *consumption* to *creativity*. Also, we will say that consumption is parallel to the scarcity described by the "Malthusian catastrophe" and creativity is parallel to the abundance described in Smith's *Wealth of Nations*. The more consumptive the activity, the lower the level to which we assign it. The more creative the activity, the higher the level to which we assign it.

Notice in Figure 17 how the different areas of being are divided into two groups, the *creation* group and the *consumptive* group.

Now notice in Figure 17 that there is a reverse order for the two groups. The highest level of creation is the spiritual, while the highest level of consumption is the mineral. The trend in creation is from the mineral to the spiritual, while the trend in consumption is from the spiritual to the mineral. Thus, when man becomes the most civilized, he will use the biggest storehouse of resources to create the smallest things in existence (Think of sub atomic particle accelerators under the Swiss Alps creating the anti-matter "God Particle"). That is a rhythmically progressing and then regressing *dynamic* world.

LEVELS of CREATION & CONSUMPTION

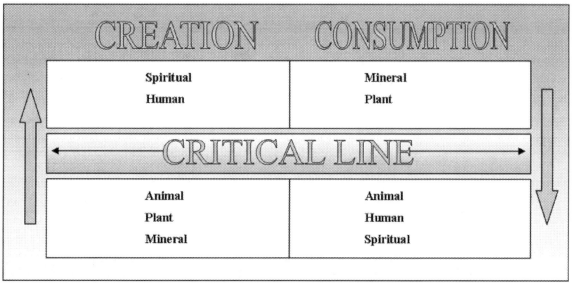

FIGURE 17

Every atom of the universe is in a constant process of change. That change has two main characteristics: creation and consumption, which go on constantly and simultaneously. This combination of activities causes growth and decay. Atoms of one element combine with atoms of another element in chemical reactions that create the molecules of chemical compounds. Then physical processes at the atomic level cause the compounds (and their molecules and their atoms) to break apart, that is, decay. They are consumed and they release energy as they are consumed.

Chemical compounds make mineral structures, which dissolve and erode. Chemical compounds in the water and air combine with mineral compounds and create plant and animal life.

From a rock to a man, I would call this life process of creation and consumption, growth and decay, birth and death, the visible, obvious, or *manifest* being. This is the physical universe up to but not including the spiritual level.

The intelligent working of theories, principles, causes and effects described by pure reason and mathematically evolving in accordance with a plan or design is the higher level of spirit. Spirit makes everything go. Spirit makes everything happen. Spirit operates logically.

As John says in his opening to his account of the Gospel, "In the beginning was the Word..." – translated as "the Word" but really being the quite untranslatable Greek word *logos* with huge connotations that mean logic, reason, order, principles, theories, essence ...*spirit* of truth and light. "...and the Word was with God and the Word was God. The same was in the beginning with God. All things were made by him (God or Logos); and without him was not anything made that was made." Einstein's vision of time as a fabric that can be folded and the eastern mystic concept that space is an astral plane and that life is a cycle are all examples of spiritual things and activities "that are neither created or destroyed (consumed)." Spiritual beings, the spirit or essence of anything, perception by the (Holy) Spirit -- this is all beyond creation and consumption, growth and decay, birth and death. This is invisible, obscure, *unmanifest* being.

To be happy, we must rise above mineral, plant, and animal concerns to a human level and then be not content with that but go farther to the spiritual level. This is the sum total of all the eras of existence. We must sharpen our understanding of manifest things to a point where we can "see through a glass darkly" and comprehend the *unmanifest* things of time, space, the Plan of Salvation, and eternal life. Then we are on the right road or "way" (Tao) to "be ye therefore perfect, even as your father which is in heaven is perfect." (Matthew 5:48)

We will never enter this state of amazing grace as long as we are fixated on consumption. We cannot suddenly disconnect ourselves from consumption, but we must constantly progress from consumption to creativity *in all our activities*.

For example, let us examine food as an area (and image) of consumption.

Plants eat (consume) minerals in order to live. Animals eat plants or other animals in order to live. Humans eat animals and plants in order to live. Humans are the only level of beings that can eat or not eat plants or animals as a *moral choice*. Early man had no problem eating animals. Indeed, early man and primitive modern man engaged in cannibalism in extreme situations as did and do various animals that will eat their own young.

Soon, however, humans learned the advantages of eating plants. Plants are found to be superior for food after the science of agriculture has progressed. Modern scientific man can understand what nutrients are in food and where they come from at the animal, plant, and even mineral level. It turns out that the building blocks of many nutrients are, in fact, minerals. Nutritious food gives animals (and, therefore, humans) life force or energy to move and use their material bodies.

Now, people living at the most advanced human level in this, the current human era, are learning how to fabricate nutrients and nutritious food without traditional agriculture and animal husbandry. Remember the story of Giri Bala, the Hindu saint? Advanced humans are on Giri's path to understanding how to get nourishment with which to operate their bodies without eating mineral rich plants or animals. There are people trying to get so excited and motivated by spiritual life that they live on spiritual food – at least as much as their still human bodies will let them. Fasting *for health* and caloric restriction make sense in a carnal, indeed obese, world. Meditation together with fasting is the primary way of spiritual life for many spiritual communities around the world and throughout the history of the world.

The point here is to rise to a higher level of existence and a better way of life than struggling to amass food, money, property, and the *things* of this world. Our goal is to rise above even the human level to a spiritual level which prepares us to leave this material world and enter a spirit world where every thought and every act is directed toward creating not consuming.

In Matthew, 6: 25 – 33, Jesus says,

> … Take no thought for your life, and what ye shall eat, or what ye shall drink; nor yet for your body, what ye shall put on. Is not the life more than meat, and the body than raiment? Behold the fowls of the air, for they sew not, neither do they reap, nor gather into barns; yet your heavenly father feedeth them. Are ye not much better than they? … And why take ye thought for raiment? Consider the lilies of the field, how they grow. They toil not, neither do they spin and yet I say unto you that even Solomon in all his Glory was not arrayed like one of these. Wherefore, if God so clothe the grass of the field, which today is and tomorrow is cast into the oven, shall he not much more clothe you, O ye of little faith? Therefore, take no thought saying what shall we eat? or what shall we drink? or wherewithal shall we be clothed? … For your heavenly father knoweth that ye have need of all these things. But seek ye first the kingdom of god and his righteousness and all these things shall be added unto you. Take, therefore, no thought for the morrow. For the morrow shall take thought for the things of itself. Sufficient unto the day is the evil thereof.

We are human beings and we live in the world. Even though our bodies are inhabited by spirit sons and daughters of heavenly father and heavenly mother, we are still mortal human beings. As human beings with the potential to be spiritual beings, we are apart from the other animals, but we are still animals. We labor to bring our bodies in subjection to our spirits. We control our appetites and our passions. We master ourselves.

All our decisions about what we will do with the earth are guided by our spirits and by the Holy Spirit. When we come to the end of the life cycle of our earth, we will move on to the spirit world and *then* we will live on cosmic energy. *Now*, we make food and drink from the good things of the earth for our wise consumption. We create the beauty of civilization. We live together in a harmonious global society. We love one another. We create heaven on earth.

Just so you know, I still eat food, but I don't spend my day thinking about food. I worked hard physically all my life doing what?...growing food. I also taught school all my life which is a more spiritual activity. I have not become a saint living on cosmic energy, but I understand the rise through the levels of existence to the highest, eternal life. At any rate, I am 91 years old sitting here working on this book.

Now let us apply to the five key human activities what we have learned about consumption at the lower levels of materialistic life and creativity at the higher levels of spiritual life. The five key human activities are: education, government, occupation, religion and communication.

CHAPTER TEN

EDUCATION

In this dynamic world, education is the most important human activity. This is so because we remember what Aristotle said. "Happiness is the rational activity of the soul in conformity with the principles of virtue." Or, to put it another way, this is so because happiness is rising through the levels of existence to the highest or spiritual level by building a life upon the experience of the eras. You cannot be happy if you do not understand what is happening to you and around you. You will be happy if you have control of your life. Being in control of your life is not getting everything you want. Self control is going in the direction that you choose. It is being in control of how you deal with your life. It is understanding yourself. "With all thy getting, get understanding." Remember?

There was a Jewish psychiatrist from Vienna (no, not Sigmund Freud. That was much earlier). This harmless, blameless man, who had amassed a great education in order that he might help people, was thrown into the Nazi death camp at Auschwitz. His name was Victor Frankl. With no medicine or even food and water, he was supposed to "care for" the sick inmates in the camp "hospital." He survived the war and wrote about his experiences in his book, *Man's Search for Meaning*. He said he learned that all he could do for the sick and dying was to help them understand what was happening to them. He counseled them on how to control their response to life and death in Auschwitz. He created a new psychotherapy that he used in his practice for the rest of his life (Yes, he used it on himself and it worked. He survived the war and had a long, *happy* life). He called it "logotherapy." He taught people, "To live is to suffer. To be happy is to find meaning in the suffering."

Education is the key. We use education to learn how to progress through the levels and build on past eras of creation and being. With education, we achieve the control over self that makes us happy. There is a lesson in every experience of the individual, personal or vicarious, direct or indirect, concrete or abstract, tangible or intangible. All experiences of the individual, no matter at what level, provide education. This education of the human individual will educate human society.

Every living creature has to learn how to live in its environment. Mastering the environment is the key to survival. Mastery of all of the levels of the environment is the key to the survival of human society. People must be educated in all of the subtle realms within the environment. They must learn the effects of the environment upon their lives, from the cosmic environment of the universe with its galaxies and star systems to the micro environment of the inner universe of cells, molecules, and atoms.

The five (metaphorical) levels of education are: mineral, plant, animal, human and spiritual.

All people receive some degree of all five levels of education at all times. When one of these levels tends to play the major role in the individual's life, it can be said that the name of this level is the name of the individual's predominant level of education at that time. For example, caveman usually had a mineral level of education. His life was often centered on activities with minerals to the point where he often worshipped the mineral *sun* in his religion.

MINERAL LEVEL OF EDUCATION

The first and lowest level of education is the first and lowest level of being, the mineral level. Metaphorically, we mean that mineral level education is the most fundamental or primary education. This is the survival education that is absorbed by the young from their parents. The young learn how to function in their environment. The young learn how to manipulate physical objects. They learn how to make use of their own bodies.

Mineral level education is practical training in the manipulation of physical objects. In mineral level education, there are no abstractions. Everything is concrete. Everything is observable cause and effect. The behavioral objective is to learn what affects you and to learn how to respond to every input. An amoeba "learns" by genetic encoding in response to stimulation how to move, what is nourishment, what will kill, etc. A lioness teaches a cub (mostly by example) how to hunt. A lion cub learns (mostly by observation and being sensitive to instinct) how to eat. A human child learns to walk, run, talk and use a toilet.

Mankind can learn to manipulate the environment by observing earthly processes at the mineral level. The dawn of technology is the dawn of the experimental method of inductive reasoning. Try it. See if that works. If it doesn't work, try something else. Try what makes sense. Keep trying until you get it right. Finally, you can do something knowing what will happen. There's nothing at stake except your life. Hence comes fire, containers, cooking, tools, weapons, shelter, clothing.

A "stone age" man can make a "mineral era" observation that the shiny black rock can be struck with the hard gray rock and little black, shiny flakes will fall off. In this way, a man can shape a spear point, a knife, and an ax. A man can then kill an animal and skin it and butcher it. Observation: friction makes heat and, therefore, a fire bow makes fire. Logical chaining of observations: An animal that cannot be caught or killed with hands and teeth alone can be first caught and then killed with tools and weapons. The animal can then be rendered into more tools, clothing, shelter, and food. Tools thus created make fire. Fire cooks food. Cooked food tastes better than uncooked food. That cooked food is nutritionally *superior* to uncooked food is a speculation upon abstractions, not observations and, therefore, not verifiable at the mineral level. In this picture we see that mineral level education (quite literally in the use of minerals) is critical to survival. The man who could not make tools and weapons and hunt with them successfully could not bring a family through life in the wild. Therefore, he could not pass his tool-weapon-hunting-building DNA to offspring.

Bring this idea of training for practical application (that is, "mineral level education") forward to modern man. Mechanically related to the principle of scientific method through experimentation is the practical principle of "troubleshooting." Today, a man can observe that his car won't start. He can inspect the engine and observe that the battery lead is corroded. He can clean the lead and start the car. All this is possible with no education beyond the mineral level. Not required is the knowledge of how electrons as sub-atomic particles make electric current and transform energy into motion. Mineral level education (practical training by observing cause and effect) is all that is required.

For cave man or rush hour man, not having an easy command of the implements of life can mean failure at best and death at worst.

In our era, at our level, we can *theorize*. We can abstract from an observable account of human life the *Theory of Instrumental Response Conditioning*. An organism (any living organism, from an amoeba to a man) is stimulated. The organism responds logically. The organism learns what the stimulus does and learns what the organism *should* do. Over time, the organism anticipates the stimulus and is ready with the correct response. Over more time, the organism develops physical attributes that better prepare it to deal with that stimulus (indeed the whole range of stimuli presented by the organism's environment).

Another way to look at mineral level education for the human being is to say that, at the mineral level, the human being learns to work with observable objects. Mankind starts out living in a cave – a cavity eroded or washed out of a rock formation. Later, people live in shelters they make of wood and hides. Still later, they can cut out, shape, and move stones to a site where they construct buildings. Forestry and carpentry evolve and wooden structures (first log, then beam, then plank, then frame) are created. Then wooden structures can be covered with earth. Then stone structures can be finished and furnished with wood. Finally, metallurgy progresses beyond tools and weapons to structural members. Then, really large stone structures are possible. Even the original land vehicles and water craft are made out of natural things fashioned to work like observable plants and animals.

The man observes the mineral and tries ways of working with it. As a result, the man responds to the experience with the mineral and is conditioned thereby. Metaphorically, the mineral teaches the man.

A pile of ore does not, of itself, have the power or ability to transform itself into metal and metallic structures. It is potential metal. Man encounters the ore and observes something that stimulates theorizing on what happens if you cook this dirt. Then the level of teaching by the mineral begins to rise. Man makes the metal. Man shapes the metal as he shaped the rock. Man learns that metal tools and weapons do things stone tools and weapons cannot do. Man finds more ores and makes more metals. Man mixes metals and improves their usefulness. Man's imagination is stimulated and man makes bigger, better, more capable metal tools, conveyances, and weapons. These metal implements give man the ability to make things of a seeming magical sophistication.

Mineral level, practical training in what can be done with what the earth will put into a man's hand is the foundation of all the higher level education people need to survive and advance to the next level of being.

Man puts a little of his human and spiritual self into the mineral material each time he learns how to do something. Each improvement or change tends to make the mineral level into a higher level of teacher, and helps to transmit a higher level of educational experience to all who come in contact with this higher level of creation. Thus, learning to manufacture, to fabricate the wherewithal of human life out of minerals is to raise the level of the educational capacity of the human race.

Therefore, we see that the business of education is a part of the total environment. Anything which exists, also teaches. There are mineral teachers, plant teachers, animal teachers, human teachers, and spiritual teachers. The higher the level of being, the higher is the level of teaching and, therefore, of education.

All creation is teaching, and all teaching is creation. To teach is to create. Each thought teaches and creates.

PLANT LEVEL OF EDUCATION

The plant level is the second level of education. Plants provide a higher quality of teaching than minerals, because, like us, plants are alive. Also, growing from a seed and dying to become soil, they teach dynamic rather than static concepts. Advancing from the mineral level to the plant level of education is good exercise for man because it stimulates growth and development. To do anything with plants, humans have to use their imagination to theorize.

Originally, humans had to deal with their fellow animals in their environment using mineral implements and structures as well as a completely physical way of observing and thinking. They didn't eat plants. They didn't wear plants. They didn't build houses out of plants. As humans learned by observing with their senses and responding to stimuli, they discovered that some plants could be eaten (for food or medicine), some could be worn, and some could be used to build things. So far, this is still in accordance with our mineral education metaphor.

But as they realized they could get more good things from plants, they observed them more closely and then they had to cross over a critical line. You couldn't figure out what plants were doing just by watching them. You had to look inside them *with your imagination*. You had to learn from what you could see and then imagine logically what you could not see. Man dealt with a living organism that cannot be built, but must be grown, that is alive until it is dead.

Man figured out how plants are born from seeds. Man did not have to find pluckable edibles. Man could plant the plants he wanted to plant. Man figured out what plants eat and how to feed them. Man figured out that sunlight gives plants energy and water is what plants are made of. Man figured out how to make (cooked) food from what he grew. Man became agricultural. Man was a farmer, a forester, a miller, a builder. Man stopped being a wanderer who lived on the land with the other animals. Now man owned land. He lived in a town, then a city. With both a mineral level and a plant level education, man formed societies that consciously thought and devised the ultimate tool for education and all that comes from education – writing.

Now man speculated as we have been speculating about this dynamic world. People reasoned and examined their feelings. They discussed. They debated and preached. In the beginning, there were no atheists and no philosophers. There were teachers of all the useful, practical arts and the theories that explained how things worked. There were preachers of what unseen forces and intelligences caused all this to be as it is. There was religion as a way to guide and direct the efforts of society. The first rulers were holy men. Later, political rulers were still appointed by the will of the Gods, not the will of the people. They were god-kings and pharaohs, the Inca, and the Emperor of Heaven.

Every mineral suggests to the human mind an image of what it is like and what it can be used for. The same is true of every plant. Thus, minerals and plants confer intelligence by being observed. For example, the rose excels in teaching lessons of beauty and scratches. The apple, peach and nut trees are outstanding in lessons of nutrition. Some plants teach lessons of medicine for sickness and some plants cause sickness. Plants teach us about appetite and addiction.

The plant is also capable of indirect teaching through the aid of other creatures. The mysterious energy of every human being is brighter when backed up by the unseen nutrients of the various plants, including nutrients that are created by the chemical reaction of sunlight with the plant. People observed that the plants are especially beneficial if they are grown without chemical additives (organic) and are eaten raw giving the consumer more cosmic energy.

Some plants are more than just teachers. The corn plant was worshipped as a kind of god by the Maya Indians of the Yucatan Peninsula. The Mayas planted, harvested, and ate corn ritualistically. When the corn died, they sometimes died. Therefore, they would give sacrifices to make the corn god happy. This plant food worship was also formed in many rice cultures of Asia (See the Chinese "Legend of the King of the Frogs" giving rice to a starving girl who then gives it to China. See the Japanese legend of "the Lord of the Bag of Rice"). Do we not have Johnny Appleseed and the forester Paul Bunyan? The metaphorical message here is that plants taught people a culture of gratitude for food.

At the mineral and plant levels of education, mankind has progressed, evolved, and developed *practically*. Man can make things out of minerals and plants. Man had to theorize *technology* in order to do this. Man became a deductive and an inductive scientist. Science is *scientia* in Latin, that is, knowledge. Man mastered inorganic chemistry (mineral level) and organic chemistry (plant level). Now, with practical, applied science and technology, man makes anything from a club to a space shuttle.

ANIMAL LEVEL OF EDUCATION

The animal level is the third level of education. Animals, as a kind of being, are much closer to humans. They are sentient individuals. While they do live by instinct with behaviors learned in the way of the "mineral level," that is, by instrumental response conditioning taught by the examples of others of their kind, still they have a measure of will, judgment, personality, and character. Animals have emotions – love, hate, fear, anger. Animals can form families, kinship groups, and herds. Animals can communicate. They can coordinate. They plan. Leaders come forth and the group intelligently follows.

In fact, when observed from Adam's point of view, very evolved animals are not far behind pre-Adamic humans in their development. In the more primitive early days of humanity, human and other animals merely preyed upon each other for food. However, as man received spirit and became a child of God, while he continued to hunt and domesticate some animals for food, he also domesticated other animals as co-workers in the tasks of life. Horses were for transportation, mules and oxen for farming, dogs and falcons for hunting, different dogs for herding and protection, and there were even animals purely for companionship. Animals are named. Animals are loved. Human life is risked to save animals and vice versa. Animals are comrades in battle and, certainly, animals (or more particularly certain qualities of certain animals) are worshipped.

The value of the animal level of education is the teaching of relationships. In our existence as animals and in our relationship with animals, we learn to identify and use our emotions. Animal level education is emotional education. At the animal level, we learn empathy and sympathy. We learn non-verbal communication, which is, of course, all that animals ever learn.

If we learn science and technology at the mineral and plant levels, then we learn art and expression at the animal level. Advanced man, functioning at the human level, tries to theorize scientifically about emotions, personality, character, will, and desire.

ART THERAPY AND DREAM SYMBOLISM INTO WORKS OF ART

…(Dr. Carl) Jung proposed that Art can be used to alleviate or contain feelings of trauma, fear, or anxiety and also to repair, restore and heal. In his work with patients and in his own personal explorations, Jung wrote that art expression and images found in dreams could be helpful in recovering from trauma and emotional distress. Jung often drew, painted, or made objects and constructions at times of emotional distress, which he recognized as recreational. (See Wikipedia: Carl Jung)

It is easy to see the value of animal level education as knowledge and mastery of the soul and of relationships through all of the arts, literature, expression of all kinds, and interpersonal relations.

HUMAN LEVEL OF EDUCATION

Here is a little recent history of the foundations of human level education.

The Neoclassical Age gave us Rene De Carte and his Cartesian plane. From that came plane, solid, and analytic geometry with its graphs of X, Y, and Z. This gave us the wave theory that would lead us to electromagnetic radiation and all electronics including telecommunications (radio, telephone, and television), not to mention atomic theory and astronomical theories. In the hands of the relativists like Einstein and Hawking, this mathematics and geometry gave us the space time continuum and the theories of astral projection.

Ancient and medieval Arabs, Persians, Indians, Greeks, Chinese and Japanese mathematicians, all worked out ways of describing points in space, areas, volumes, coordinates, and values changing over time and distance with their algebra, geometry, and trigonometry. All of this would make possible understanding of the stars, planets, galaxies and the universe as well as navigation over the surface of our own earth.

Isaac Newton was the apex of the Neoclassical Period and a transition into the *Age of Reason*, also known as *the Enlightenment*. He took all of the mathematics and science that had been done and came forth with Calculus and Newtonian Physics. With those things came buildings, machinery, travel, and industry that would vaunt us into our modern age.

At the same time Van Leeuwenhoek made parallel discoveries in light and optics that helped aging human eyes but also allowed us to teleport our vision out into space with his *telescope* where we could validate the star theories of the ancients and the moderns. He also revealed a new *micro-universe* of tiny structures with his *microscope*. From this would come our validation of cells, molecules, and, with a little help from physics…atoms.

The human level is the fourth level of education, but not the highest level. Human beings are frequently referred to as puny and insignificant as they spread out on the face of the mountains, deserts, and oceans. Human beings cannot compete with animals on a level of purely physical attainments, but humans can utterly dominate all species and all environments because humans can communicate abstractions to humans they will never see. Humans can cooperate and coordinate on a tribal, national, regional, and, rarely, global level.

Other animals can do a little primitive, mineral level building and tool using, but only humans can explode things, drain whole basins, flood whole valleys, move mountains, move bodies of water, cover terrain with plants, or denude an entire landscape of plants. Whatever animals have done physically through evolution, man has learned how to build machines to do with God given mind gifts. Birds can fly but humans can build flying machines that carry many people to the edge of the atmosphere. Whales can dive deep and stay down a long time but a nuclear powered submarine can dive deeper and go around the world submerged.

The human level of education gives man the ability to make physical that which he has conceived in his imagination. He can abstract from the experience of his five senses visions of things he will never see, echoes of things he will never hear, and the texture of things he will never touch.

Humans can use mathematics and science to posit things in outer space, inner space, inside themselves, and on other planes of existence. They can describe how electricity absolutely has to work and build a generator and a motor based on what they imagined and, lo, it works. They can describe an electronic process like telecommunication and build vacuum tubes and then semiconductors and then solid state, digital transistors and, lo, they build a computer which is a mechanical replica of their own brains and they didn't even know that until they started talking about their brains "accessing" information that had been "saved" by "programs."

At the mineral and plant levels, humans use materials found in nature to fashion their physical environment. At the human level of education, they decide what materials will build the environment they imagine and then they create materials that do not exist in nature, like plastic, artificial fabrics, composite fibers, glass, metal alloys, plasma, liquid crystal.

At the mineral and plant level, humans liberate energy in mechanical ways no animal ever did or ever will with fire, solar collection, friction, steam, internal combustion, and wind collection to name the traditional ones. At the human level of education, humans understand the most advanced abstract theories of energy liberation and use. Humans can liberate nuclear energy, both fission and fusion. They can harness the power of magnetism. Humans flirt with "warping" the time space continuum.

The human level of education has made possible manipulations of life that enhance the benefits of nature. We can genetically engineer crops. We can map DNA and selectively breed animals and people to the point of mutation. We are on the verge of cloning. We can re-program the functions of stem cells to grow replacement organs and tissue. What a reptile can do naturally when it re-grows a tail, we can now do consciously when we grow a disease free liver or other organ.

The human level of education has given us ever more God-like power, but not necessarily God-like judgment. Climate damage, climate repair, climate control, destroying species, saving species, filling the earth with people, emptying the earth of people -- Our practical and technical capabilities are so advanced that they can literally change the world.

SPIRITUAL LEVEL OF EDUCATION

The spiritual level of education is the fifth level. Just as plants are something more than minerals, animals are something more than plants, and humans are something more than animals; so spiritual beings are something more than humans. This *something more* continually increases as one goes up the ladder of growth.

In the United States, church and state are legally separated, because a majority cannot agree upon crucial issues. Many of these differences are small, but the average person lacks the insight and compassion to give in on these minor points which prevent unification of church and state. As a result our young people suffer from this lack of prayer and meditation, and turn to drugs, sex and violence instead. These prevent the level of consciousness from rising and education suffers. There is also a great loss in health, money and environment.

At the other levels there was intelligence. At the spiritual level, there is *wisdom*. Now we pass scientia (knowledge), practe (skill), and techne (theory) and go on to *sophia* (wisdom). *Philosophy* is "love of wisdom." Mankind rose through the various levels of observation and contemplation of life in the world.

For all their theorizing, experimenting, building, repairing, and troubleshooting, people could not find the *mind* in the *brain*. They could not find the "heart" in the heart. What happened *exactly* when a living organism died? What does that mean died *exactly*? Was the alive part extinguished? Or was it gone? If it was gone, where did it go? And what was *it*? What makes people happy? not gratified, not satiated, not relaxed, but happy.

A whole new science grew up called *social science*. Social science is concerned with social justice, social engineering, social "norms." And what is normal? What is the scale? What is the spectrum? "Social" was a secular humanist way of trying to use science to determine values? By the way, what is a "secular humanist?" Is there such a thing as a "religious humanist?" It turns out there is. More on this to come.

Philosophers

Philosophy had done much more than social science to rationally discover human values. Socrates taught us to know ourselves. He taught us to never say we knew a thing when we did not know it, but had only been told it.

Plato taught us the idea of forms. There is an abstract set of attributes for good, for beauty, for right. There is a form of the good. Plato was on to something. When he said form, he meant spirit.

Aristotle took it further. "Happiness is the rational activity of the *soul* in conformity with the principles of virtue." Aristotle's major contribution may have been his book entitled *Ethics*. There, he explained "The Golden Mean." For every type of human behavior there is a spectrum of responses to a situation. The correct, the "right" response is never the extreme, but the wisest and best and most effective behavior in between the two extremes. For example, in between foolhardy recklessness on one hand and craven panic on the other hand, *somewhere* in there (depending on the situation) is *courage*.

Emmanuel Kant issued his "Categorical Imperative: No person should be treated only as a means but also always as an end." Again, philosophy is groping toward spirituality. Kant's Categorical imperative is perilously close to Jesus' Golden Rule: "Do unto others as you would have others do unto you."

In the place that, today, we call north China, where, in 500 B.C. there were only warring kingdoms, there was a wandering professor/preacher who tried to get the kings and their courts to listen to him. He was kind of a combination of Socrates and John the Baptist. In a Romanization of his Chinese name, he was K'ung Fu Tzu. Tzu means "master" as in teacher (Remember the Hindu yogi?). Remember that Jesus was "master" to his disciples. They learned his "discipline." Rabbi means master/teacher. Jesus was a rabbi. Throughout the world, the inculcators of new thought who challenge people to find out the truth are always educators. K'ung Fu Tzu – Master K'ung Fu -- in the latinization of his name -- was Confucius.

Confucius, like Aristotle, taught a well worked out doctrine of ethics. Like all philosophers and teachers, he found himself groping for first causes. Why are things the way they are? Who are we? Where did we come from? Why are we here? Where are we going? What is absolute good? What is absolutely the right thing to do? Why does a good person trying to do right always encounter opposition? What (or who) is this evil willed opposition?

Like his western counterparts, Confucius tried to answer all those questions logically, using human experience he knew about. But, like his western counterparts, he had the integrity to realize that he must seek the spirit of things. He must get at the essence of things. The Taoists and the Buddhists have more answers to questions of spirits and eternity and God than does Confucius. Still, Confucian ethics appeal to the ultimate judge of truth that is "heaven." Confucius urged the warring, north Chinese states to unite under a "celestial empire" or a "celestial kingdom" that would have the "Mandate of Heaven."

Confucius was more comfortable applying his assumed first principles to human conduct. He gave an emotional, spiritual tone to his definitions and rules. Confucius is all about love, respect, honor, and harmony.

There are thinkers and teachers east and west, but their skill, technology, and knowledge do not satisfy the person who is afraid of love and death. Morality has been called "the science of ought's." Technical constructions of moral codes, however, do not satisfy. People yearn to see not just what is right but also what is righteous. They are terrified not so much of what is incorrect, but rather of what is evil.

The classic thinkers of Greece and Rome tried to explain

➢ *anima* – in Greek: *psyche* (vital force or soul; the mysterious thing in us that makes us alive rather than dead; animation),
➢ *corpus* (physical body),
➢ *mortalis* (mortality; the ability of life to die),
➢ *spiritus* (spirit; the person from a pre-existence who first inhabits and then departs the physical body), and, of course,
➢ *mens* (Latin for mind – mental, etc.) Not to be confused with brain. Mind is the contents of the brain. Mind is a *persona* (person; personality) proceeding in accordance with logos; thinking logically and rationally (or illogically and irrationally in the grip of passionate emotions) in accordance with mental processes. Mental processes cannot be found let alone measured physiologically.

Readers will recall that Carl Jung is a primary source and influence on this work. *Wikipedia* digests the great biographies of Jung such as *Carl Jung; Wounded Healer of the Soul: an Illustrated Biography* by Claire Dunne, *Jung: A Biography* by Deidre Bair, and *A Life of Jung* by Ronald Heyman . I integrate many Jungian concepts into my understanding of religion, my understanding of a spirituality that describes the universe in various helpful ways, and my utilitarian philosophy of life in service. I do these things, just as Jung himself did.

Carl Jung and his friend and rival, Sigmund Freud, are the pioneers of psychiatry, but whereas Freud examined mental processes looking for causes and cures of mental illness, Jung looked for the way spirit worked with mind to express soul. Freud studied disease. Jung preached health.

> Quoting from *Wikipedia*,
>
> …Jung's school was *analytical psychology*, later called simply Jungian psychology a la Freudian psychology. Jung's approach to psychology has been influential in counter-culture movements across the globe. Jung is considered as the first modern psychologist to state that the human psyche is "by nature religious." He emphasized understanding the psyche through exploring the worlds of dreams, art, mythology, religion, and philosophy…
>
> …Although he was a theoretical psychologist and practicing clinician, much of his life's work was spent exploring other areas, including Eastern and Western philosophy, alchemy, astrology, and sociology, as well as literature and the arts. His most notable ideas include the concept of psychological *archetypes*, the *collective unconscious*, and *synchronicity*…
>
> …Jung emphasized the importance of balance and harmony. He cautioned that modern people rely too heavily on science and logic and would benefit from integrating spirituality and appreciation of unconscious realms. He considered the process of *individuation* necessary for a person to become whole. This is a psychological process of integrating the conscious with the unconscious while still maintaining conscious autonomy…
>
> …Jung visited India. His experience in India led him to become fascinated and deeply involved with Hindu philosophy, helping him form key concepts, including integrating spirituality into daily life and appreciation of the unconscious…
>
> …Jung (had an) … interest in reports of flying saucers…
>
> …Jung's work on himself and his patients convinced him that life has a spiritual purpose beyond material goals. Our main task, he believed, is to discover and fulfill our deep innate potential, much as the acorn contains the potential to become the oak, or the caterpillar to become the butterfly. Based on his study of Christianity, Hinduism, Buddhism, Gnosticism, and Taoism, as well as other traditions, Jung perceived that this journey of transformation, that is, individuation, is at the mystical heart of all religions. It is a journey to meet the self and at the same time to meet the Divine. Unlike Sigmund Freud, Jung thought spiritual experience was essential to our well-being…
>
> …Jung's primary disagreement with Freud stemmed from their differing concepts of the unconscious. Jung saw Freud's theory of the unconscious as incomplete and unnecessarily negative. According to Jung (though not according to Freud), Freud conceived the unconscious solely as a repository of repressed emotions and desires. Jung agreed with Freud's model of the unconscious, what Jung called the 'personal

unconscious,' but he also proposed the existence of a second, far deeper form of the unconscious underlying the personal one. This was the collective unconscious, where the archetypes themselves resided, represented in mythology (and legend captured in literature and art as well as codes of belief)...

Spirituality as a cure for alcoholism

...Jung recommended spirituality as a cure for alcoholism and he is considered to have had an indirect role in establishing *Alcoholics Anonymous*. Jung's influence can sometimes be found in more unexpected quarters. For example, Jung once treated an American patient ... suffering from chronic alcoholism. After working with the patient for some time and achieving no significant progress, Jung told the man that his alcoholic condition was near to hopeless, save only the possibility of a spiritual experience. Jung noted that occasionally such experiences had been known to reform alcoholics where all else had failed...

The influence of Jung thus indirectly found its way into the formation of Alcoholics Anonymous, the original twelve-step program, and from there into the whole twelve-step recovery movement, although AA as a whole is not Jungian and Jung had no role in the formation of that approach or the twelve steps...

Lord Siddhartha left his palace and wandered the Indian sub continent inquiring, experiencing, meditating, and praying until he achieved enlightenment. He could then proclaim to others the way of life *about which he had been told by the cosmos itself.* Today there are millions of people who do miraculous things because of the "reverence for life" they obtained from "the Enlightened One."

A young merchant of Mecca, Mohammed, became weary of the wrangling of the world and went to a cave overlooking the city where he meditated and prayed. He recorded how he was visited by angels (heavenly messengers, remember?) and taught true religion. He learned of the one God, the true and living God. His record became the holy scripture of his new faith. He came out of the cave into a life of prosyletizing, politics, and war to put on the earth what he had been shown in the cave.

Interesting how, about 900 years before Mohammed, Plato wrote an allegory to express his philosophy of life wherein some people have been imprisoned *in a cave* for their whole lives and know nothing of the world or life except what their senses tell them. Being human, though, they are curious. Also, they understand that they are suffering. They explore the dark cave looking for something better. They see light. They go to the light and cross over a *critical line* (italics mine, terminology his) and discover the world and the life outside the cave. This is their revelation. Plato's metaphor of "sense people" and "understanding" people is, I believe, parallel to my metaphor for humans rising through the levels to achieve a spiritual understanding of the universe outside their little environment.

The Greek word for *revelation* is *epiphany*. Everybody needs epiphany. You can't know, really know, anything without a spiritual witness that the thing you think is, is. Even scientists, maybe especially scientists, need epiphany – revelation. The Greek scientist Archimedes had an epiphany when he solved an important problem and he cried out "Eureka!" meaning "I found it!" Revelation is a Latin word meaning something that is revealed, become visible, and brought to light.

Spirituality is connecting our spirit self to the unseen spiritual world that is out there in the space time continuum, on other worlds, on some other astral plane that people all over the Earth in all traditions call "heaven" or "the Celestial Empire" or "paradise."

In the *Yoga* (disciplines, doctrines, "schools") of Hinduism, if we are sensitive through meditation and opening to life, we will see a big change coming. In eastern (and western) astrology, the solar/astral cycle swings us through a wave of dark evil to light good to dark evil to light good and so on. The avatars come to us in dark times and show us the light outside the cave of ignorance, selfishness, and cruelty. According to sources as disparate as the Yogi of India, the New Age Aquarians, the Zoroastrian *"Wise* Men," the Prophet Isaiah, the Prophet Mohammed, and the Savior of the World, we are coming out of the dark into the light. We must go through a cataclysm in the "last days" of the old era and the "new day" of the new era.

When the spiritual level of education is reached, there will be almost no sickness. Holistic living will prevent such things. Instead of educating good doctors to care for illnesses, we will educate good pupils who don't get sick and need a doctor's care. Crime and war will not exist. Poverty will be unknown. Science will tap the sun's abundant energy supply without any pollution. The necessities of life will become as free and plentiful as the air one breathes.

To achieve such things there must be a great unification of government, science, religion and thought of all kind. Man's mode of living will become as harmonious as a great symphony orchestra. Billions now spent to keep people apart will be invested to bring them together to explore the spiritual realm.

When we have done all that we can do with reason, logic, and practical skill, then we break through to a whole new level of achievement which can only be reached with spiritual effort. This is the Spiritual Era where we function at the spiritual level as a result of spiritual education. All truth is then gathered into one whole *science and religion of life.*

LEVELS OF EDUCATION

SPIRITUAL

HUMAN

ANIMAL

PLANT

MINERAL

FIGURE 18

CHAPTER ELEVEN
GOVERNMENT

Now let us examine government through the Eras at the various levels in order to identify the trends within the trend of all trends. Let us find the highest and best government in the Spiritual Era at the Spiritual Level. Like Plato's cave people, we want to cross over the critical line of second best level to the very best level of government. In government as in all things, we want to pass from dark to light.

At the lowest level of government and life, no humans are in control. The animal laws, such as survival of the fittest, are in force. The ultimate goal for human life is to have *all* in control. This is a level of law and life where man neither rules himself nor anyone else.

MINERAL LEVEL OF GOVERNMENT

Plato is channeling racial memory when he sets his allegory of man's progress in a cave. Pre-Adamic humans, like many of their fellow animals, lived in caves. They lived in families who made a family home together. As the family extended, there came to be clans. Soon, clans claimed all the caves in an area. Then clans worked together in kinship groups to dominate a territory. Finally, there were enough social units throughout a region to create tribes. Tribes evolved languages, customs, beliefs, laws, and lawgivers. The lawgiver was a decider of questions about what the tribe should do. The lawgiver was a judge who would choose between options or positions. Thus, this tribal leader ruled or judged the people.

Originally, in the first families, this ruler – judge – lawgiver was the man who created the family. Father was the leader. Father had authority because father was responsible. The family looked to father to lead them in the hunt, to lead them in the fight. No man who could not hunt and fight and build could have a family.

Father led the family. Mother ran the home. Mother ruled over the children. Father educated the sons. Mother educated the daughters. This simple patriarchal order expanded out to the larger social units. Eventually, an increasingly sophisticated division of labor brought about war chiefs (captains), talking chiefs (diplomats, emissaries), and judges (as in the *Book of the Judges* in the *Old Testament* or "jefe" or "sheikh" or "het man" or "chief").

Many times, mother had sensitivity and an awareness of unseen things that were valuable to a man who would listen to a woman. Women could divine the message of the stars, the wind, the dead, the neighbors. Tribes had women soothsayers, oracles, casters of the runes. Eventually, grandmother could be as potent as grandfather and some societies became matriarchies rather than patriarchies.

From the 12 tribes of Israel to the 29 tribes of Ishmael, from the clans of Scotland to the "Indians" of America, to the Amazon to Iraq to the Viet-Lao Highlands to New Guinea, the tribal way has always been and still is a good way, but it can never rise above the mineral level of government.

MINERAL LEVEL OF GOVERNMENT

Again, the tower of Babel is a wonderful metaphor for the inability of the tribal way to construct a society of mineral buildings, tools, and weapons as well as plant agriculture and animal husbandry.

After the experience of the tower of Babel, whatever, whenever and wherever that literally was, cities appeared. Tribes lived off the land high in the mountains, out on the plains, deep in the jungles, and far out in the deserts. Cities, however, collected the products of agriculture, animal husbandry, and industry. Cities were situated on key terrain - -the confluence of rivers and the intersection of natural trade routes; natural harbors and passages through natural barriers. Cities grew up around sacred places where people could serve a god. When all these other requirements had been fulfilled, the city had a lot to lose and so it was situated on defensible terrain.

Cities were fed by the people in satellite villages and on the land around the city. The people on the land found their efforts organized, utilized, rewarded, exploited, and protected by the authorities in the city. This meant that cities could not be governed in the tribal way. Cities had to leave behind the mineral level and embrace the plant level of human development.

In the tribal way, people understood the universe with the aid of holy men and holy women. Soothsayers, prophets, spiritual mediums, and all other interpreters of the universe to mankind educated the people in mineral level spirituality. This mineral level spirituality was the best they could do for science and philosophy.

But this was not enough for the city. In the plant level city, there grew up *religion* and *priests*. Priests could explain to the people how the universe worked and how life on earth worked. Priests were astronomers, botanists, physicians, and scholars. They officiated and explained all of the passages of life.

But priests could not rule. Some tried, but, in the end, theocracy did not have the right skill set. There had to be a *law giver*. There had to be a secular, practical, technical, manager of the activities of the city state. This lawgiver, however, had to be sufficiently spiritual and, indeed, faithful to god or the gods to govern the city in a moral and ethical way (as supervised by the priests).

The city needed a king who would be a skilled manager and an exalted ruler. Also, in order to tell the people the story of life and the will of god in order that they might understand their instructions for doing what they had to do, There had to be writing. Why? Why does there have to be writing in a true city? Because a city is a center of civilization, that's why. What is civilization? The Latin word *civis* means a "citizen", that is, someone who lives together with other people civilly, with civility. There is a denotative meaning to civilization: people (citizens) living together with sophisticated division of labor requiring indirect and even mass communication, i.e. writing.

All over the post Babel world, between 3000 and 4000 B.C., Cities grew up at river mouths, overlooking mountain passes, and on giant crossroads with pyramids, ziggurats, temples, royal palaces, military citadels, marketplaces, legislative chambers, courts, libraries, schools, and homes of all these city people - - these citizens - -who worked in all these places and made them run right. They did their jobs because they could communicate with each other and coordinate their activities *in writing*.

Sitting in his palace on top of the hill in the middle of the city right next to the temple was the god – king or godly anointed king surrounded by priestly scribes such as King Nammu of Ur, King Hammurabi of Babylon, Pharoah in Egypt, Montezuma of Tenochtitlan, and Ch'in of the forbidden city of Peking. This is a government of weight and force. It is the level where one mind is the collective mind of all. The laws emanate from one lawgiver to all subjects. The ruler has been sent to the people by the Gods or by God or by Heaven. The ruler is proclaimed by the priests to *be God*. These are the plant level cities of plant level civilization.

ANIMAL LEVEL OF GOVERNMENT

Government evolved beyond city states with god-kings, priests, and city dwellers supplied by agricultural tribes. At the animal level, people were concerned with the structure of relationships. Building on the birth and growth of ancient civilizations, The classic civilizations of Greece, Rome, China, India, Arabia, and Meso-America appeared and rose to their great heights. They went so far because of their understanding of critical principles.

In the west, they learned that government should not be politics. *Politics* is a Greek descended word meaning "having to do with the Polity." *Polity* is a Greek descended word meaning something like "having to do with the people who live in the polis." *Polis* is a Greek word meaning "the state - -understood to be the city state." Literally, Polis is a hilltop or a commanding height, because all Greek city states were built on hilltops. From these Greek concepts we get our words politics, politician, policy, police, metropolitan, and polemic. All of this would seem to indicate that politics *is* government.

However, the original government of the Greek city states was like that of the ancient civilizations we have examined. They had *monarchy* (Greek for "one orderer" or "one ruler"). A king was blessed by the priests of the patron god or goddess of the city state. The king ruled in accordance with customs that had the force of law handed down *to the priests* from an unknown past. Later, weak kings became tools in the hands of priest factions representing different gods. Different factions had different sets of ideas or *ideologies*. Then the powerful warriors and landowners moved in to rule by a council of the few most powerful or *oligarchy*.

When the oligarchs persuaded their followers in the polity ("body politic") to back their *policy* for government, political factions were created and politics diverged from government.

The word government comes from the Latin word *gubernator*. A gubernator is the "helmsman" who steers a ship. The helmsman is not the captain, the ultimate legitimate authority, but the helmsman is in control of the ship. If the helmsman wants the ship to go one way and the captain wants it to go another way, then the only way the captain or anyone else on board can force the helmsman to obey orders is to take the helmsman away from the helm of the ship.

This is our figurative image for impeachment or revolution or other overthrow of the government. Of course, there might be a peaceful, legitimate way to get the helm away from the helmsman and put the captain in control of a new helmsman. That would be the idea of choosing rulers. If the people choose (Latin: elect) by voting (Latin: wishing), then the people (Greek: demos) are the captain of the ship or the ruler (Greek: critos). Thus, the people rule (*democracy*).

Over the centuries of western civilization, we have this image of the government guiding the "ship of state" in accordance with the orders of the "captain," who is the image of the final legitimate authority in the state.

This authority may be the monarch who has been placed on his or her throne by God to rule in God's way and protect the people from unruly *factions*. On the other hand, the monarch may be a tyrant (Greek: usurper; he who takes over and that brutally, oppressively) and so the people unite and turn things over or turn things around (Latin: revolution), establishing a democracy but maintaining laws to control factions. An example would be the Romans throwing out King Tarquin "the Proud" and setting up a new government without a king ordained by priests.

This new setup has to have a written (or unwritten) *constitution* (Latin: "construction; edifice; something built") that establishes a *republic* (from Latin: *res publica* meaning literally "public thing;" denotatively: "common wealth" or, in old English, "common weal;" that is, common wellness or health).

This authority may be God or the Gods who has or have revealed his/her/their will to the people through priests who act in the name of God. That would be a *theocracy* (Greek: rule by God)

But one way or another, a legitimate government runs things in accordance with accepted rules. These rules are believed by the people to be the way the Earth and the universe in which the Earth moves are *governed*.

By the end of the Animal Era, pagan, slavery supported, "classic" civilizations were politically clever, but governmentally unintelligent. They had a tremendous reach, but no visionary grasp. Empires ruled from the center for the benefit of the center.

Their time was the "meridian of time," when the Savior of the World was fore-ordained to come. They ignored him until they killed him. They had no idea what he meant to them. They persecuted the Church of Jesus Christ and its "citizens" the Saints. Having given up their republics with their constitutions and rights and elections, they had gone back to god-kings and subjects serving the great city. They had lost their animal vigor.

The great mass of humanity outside the classical world was functioning in a mishmash of mineral, plant, and animal levels. They were tribal, hunter-gatherer-pastoral, worshipped spirits of land, sky, and animals, and lusted for the accumulated *things* of the great empires and their cities.

The Western Roman Empire fell to Goths and Huns and Vandals. The Eastern Roman Empire hung on until Arabs burst out of Arabia and spread over the Hellenistic world, detaching it from the Christian Greek "Roman" rulers of the great city of Constantinople ("Constantine's Polis").

The Muslim Arabs rose to great heights of culture, technology, and spirituality and then were themselves dragged down by successive waves of conquerors from Turkey and Mongolia.

The Romans destroyed the Great Temple and the holy city of Jerusalem and drove the Jews out of their country, not to return for 1900 years.

Huns conquered the Ch'in dynasty and, later, Manchu's conquered the Qing ("Ching") dynasty.

Aztecs conquered the Mayans and, much later, the Spanish conquered the Aztecs.

All of these people fell from an advanced *classical age* into a *dark age*.

Christians endured this anti – civilization chaos while looking forward to the second coming of Christ. In his second epistle to the Thessalonians (2 THS 2:3), the Apostle Paul foretold this "Great Apostasy" when he wrote, "let no man deceive you by any means: for that day shall not come except there be a falling away first and that man of sin be revealed, the son of perdition."

After 900 years of Christianized feudalism in the west and the rise of new dynasties in the empires of the east, there was a rebirth (a "renaissance") of all the good things from the classical era and a flowering of new ways into a modern era. This dynamic world had completed another cycle and moved from the Age of Chivalry to the Age of Reason, from the animal to the human level of government.

HUMAN LEVEL OF GOVERNMENT

At the human level, government became a science, called *political science*. In the terminology of the development of western civilization, this has been called the "Early Modern Period" and the "Rise of the Nation State." Human level government was theorized by Plato in his book, *The Republic* and by Aristotle in his book, *Politics*.

Plato describes an ideal nation state that is ruled by *aristocrats* (Aristocracy is Greek: "rule by the best people"). At their head is a "philosopher king" who has no political concerns because, as king ruler, he has no unmet needs and does not need to work politically to maintain himself in power. He has mastered all the arts and sciences of government and sees that the best state gives him and everybody else the best life. The philosopher king is the supreme manager and administrator. He is a "technocrat."

For Aristotle, human level politics is "...the connection between the well-being of the political community and that of the citizens who make it up, his belief that citizens must actively participate in politics if they are to be happy and virtuous, and his analysis of what causes and prevents revolution within political communities... (He has) been a source of inspiration for many contemporary theorists..." (*Encyclopedia of Philosophy*)

The human level of government begins with the Late Medieval Period, also known as the High Middle Ages (the beginning of the 14th century) when the great universities of England and Europe from Cambridge and Oxford to Paris and Pisa encouraged those old priest scribes to become professors of Aristotle and Plato, Virgil and Cicero.

Around the year 1300, tremendous things happened in the west. Marco Polo came home to Venice from China, bringing spaghetti, gunpowder, block printing, silk, and knowledge of a fabulous "celestial empire." After 300 years, the crusades were pretty much over. While it is true that the Christians had desired mightily to crush Islam and liberate the holy land, it is also true that, almost against their cherished instincts, they lived in harmony among the Muslims and the Jews and brought back huge ideas and wonderful technology in mathematics, science, medicine, and community organization.

In fact, Muslim Arab scholars had preserved for the Europeans all of the learning of the Greeks. When the barbarians raged through the Roman Empire and their descendants built feudal Christian Europe, all of the subtlety of the Greeks was in an Arab "safe deposit box." Just by the way, when the Irish were being converted to Christianity, they embraced all the learning of the Romans and preserved it from the ravages of the barbarians until their beloved church was ready to re-disseminate it from the church run universities.

This intellectual replanting prompted the Renaissance. The Renaissance gave us

➤ Painting, sculpture, and architecture that praised humanity and showed the god level potential of human beings. Renaissance art captured spirituality.

➤ Copernicus and Galileo, who taught us the solar system and suggested the universe beyond.

➤ Christopher Columbus, who validated the mathematical-geographic theories of the Greeks about the shape and size of the Earth and opened the *Age of Exploration* which became the *Age of Imperialism,*

➤ Marco Polo and others who did on land what Columbus did on the sea.

➤ Alighieri Dante who elevated poetry to philosophical discourse and invented introspective narrative of the self, thus helping Columbus and others launch the *Age of Individualism.*

➤ Leonardo Da Vinci who expanded the profession of inventor. Leonardo may be the "father of machinery."

➤ William Shakespeare, who is a transcendent figure in literature. He created a theater of the whole human being that is completely relevant in all times and places. Whoever we are, he tells our story.

➤ Niccolo Machiavelli who, in his one big book, *The Prince,* taught statecraft for the modern era. We do not *accept* "Machiavellian" ways, but we know we have to *deal* with Machiavellian ways. Machiavelli collides with Aristotle to produce Benjamin Franklin, Abraham Lincoln, Franklin Roosevelt, and Winston Churchill.

➤ *Saint* Thomas Moore, *Rabbi* Baruch (sometimes called Benedict) Espinoza, and Erasmus of Rotterdam, co-founders of *humanism.* They insisted that government, church, and society treat people humanly and humanely. They believe in the worth and freedom of the human individual. They start the line of *religious humanism.* In the 20th century would come *secular humanism.*

➤ All of the above inspire *the Age of Individualism,* which would give rise to competition, individual excellence, individual goal setting, and self actualization, self absorption, self righteousness, and self respect, all for better or for worse.

From the Renaissance came, inevitably, a *Neo* (Greek: new) classical Age. In the 17th century, this neoclassical age produced the nation state we know today with governmental forms we still use, such as parliamentary debate and procedure, ministers, international law and treaties, a judicial system we would recognize today – either in the form of judge and jury with rules of evidence and protection of rights or in the form of a panel of judges and administrative rather than judicial procedures. Neoclassical states in the west had professional armies and navies, diplomatic corps, and bureaucracies.

They also had kings and nobles. Feudalism clashed with modernity. Established churches established ideologies. The English Civil War was fought by Puritan religious fanatics who were also believers in modern parliamentary government and late feudal royalists who were more rational about religion but less rational about government. Modernity and piety won. Oliver Cromwell ordered the beheading of the king, Charles I. Oliver Cromwell had engraved on his own tomb, "Christ, not man, is king."

The Thirty Years War (1618-1648) was religious war between Lutheran Protestants of North Germany and Roman Catholics of South Germany to be sure but it was also a political war between modernity and the medieval past – bustling cities and ports making money with a practical religion against land owning nobles serving a Holy Roman (Austrian) Empire and served by a people controlling church.

Renaissance and Neo-classicism set the stage for the 18th century *Age of Reason* also known as *The Enlightenment*. This is the time that carried the current of the renaissance and the neoclassical age out to their logical extremes. In the days of Plato and Aristotle, there had been only philosophy - -the love of wisdom. 2000 years later, there was also natural philosophy (Newtonian physics), economic philosophy (the mercantilism of Jean Baptiste Colbert, "Chief Minister" to King Louis XIV of France and the capitalism of Adam Smith in his *Wealth of Nations*), and now...*political philosophy*.

Political philosophy in the Age of Reason wanted whatever was natural. But what is natural? All the political philosophers agreed that mankind lived in a state of nature.

Perhaps the greatest political philosopher of the Age of Reason was Voltaire. His life spanned almost the complete 18th century - - from the beginning to the end of the Age of Reason. He said that nature is a universe based on reason. Voltaire said the reasonable man respects nature.

Thomas Hobbes wasn't so sure. The life of Hobbes bestrode the end of the new classical age and the beginning of the Age of Reason. Hobbes said that a state of nature was a state of animalistic chaos. Beasts lived in the wilderness in a state of nature. Hobbes was aligned with what we have called the animal level. Hobbes said that, in a state of nature, a man survived "by the strength of his own right arm." Also, he said, in a state of nature, a man's life was "nasty, brutish, and short."

Government, Hobbes proclaimed, must make a clearing in the wilderness where the sun of enlightenment would make all bright and warm. Government must be a huge and powerful *leviathan* (the "800 pound gorilla in the room" as we say today) that can force citizens to treat each other in a human and humane manner, in accordance with reasonable and enlightened principles. Hobbes said that this leviathan would be the *sovereign* power of the nation state. A moral and ethical sovereign was critical to "refereeing" the great game of life between human beings that are naturally cruel and selfish.

God granted the sovereign an absolute understanding of true principles of right and wrong, justice and injustice, good and evil. The law of the land was extracted by the sovereign from divine law. Animalistic man, the natural man, needed to be hedged about with laws. Big government was good. Hobbes was comfortable with the "philosopher king" of Plato's *Republic*.

Jean Jacques Rousseau was excited by the state of nature. He liked animal freedom and exuberance. He wandered Europe from one exuberant sexual experience to another and thought that was what living naturally was all about. He never strayed into a real wilderness or dealt with any real beasts, human or otherwise. Rousseau thought that nature and natural law were the creations of nature's god. Rousseau thought that natural law gave the natural man natural rights. Rousseau thought that it was unnatural and immoral to inhibit man's natural curiosity, creativity, and productivity. The law of the land was extracted by the people from natural law. Little government was good and no government would be better if all men were as reasonable as Jean Jacques Rousseau. Rousseau enjoyed the uncomfortable dialogs of Socrates.

Hobbes worried about security. Rousseau lusted for freedom.

In between was John Locke. Locke continued the English tradition of determination to protect rights. Locke reasoned on the rights conferred by Magna Carta and the English Bill of Rights. He said that the rights conferred by nature all revolved around individual rights to life, liberty, and property.

Huge concepts of government piled up like a storm tide at the end of the Age of Reason. God kings, churchly scribes, monarchy, oligarchy, aristocracy, democracy, voting in elections, orthodoxy, theocracy, constitutional republics, lawmakers and lawgivers, rights and duties, the Athenian way, the Roman way, the Saxon English way, the chivalric feudal European way… The wave had to break. At the end of the century, at the end of the age, there were two giant and very different *revolutions*.

The French Revolution was a radical revolution. The people fought to gain rights they had never had. The American Revolution was a conservative revolution. The people fought to keep rights they had always had. The French Revolution began with a *Declaration of the Rights of Man* and ended in a "Reign of Terror." The American Revolution began with a *Declaration of Independence* and ended with a Constitutional Convention.

The French Revolution began with a spirit of brotherly love and a feeling of opportunity to make wrong things right. It quickly descended into hysteria, fanaticism, and paranoia. It started with noble aspirations for freedom and justice, but it ended with a bloody lust for vengeance and elimination of political rivals.

It would be dishonorable and inaccurate to say that there was no score settling or politics by murder in the American Revolution. However, those unjustifiable ways of conducting revolutionary war were never policy nor were they even condoned by revolutionary leaders.

We must remember that the French people and even the French intellectuals of the Enlightenment had no practical experience with the human level of government. They had among them political philosophers. Therefore, they could make political factions out of their political theories. However, none of them had ever been an executive, a legislator, or a judge.

All of the American people and especially the American intellectuals who led the revolution came from 150 years of experience of self government under the British Constitution.

The critical difference between the two revolutions, however, was that the French Revolution spent its spiritual energy hating the church and, therefore, had no interest in God while the American Revolution was carried out by people who had come to America *because* of their belief in God. The French did not understand what the English Puritans meant when they equated human and godly as well as inhuman and ungodly. The French revolutionaries thought that cutting the heads off the children of aristocrats was logically demanded by their situation. They mocked as weak, illogical, and counterrevolutionary the idea that they were evil, satanic, and *inhuman*.

Napoleon took the spirit of the French revolution and made it rational and practical. He used its ideals to excite the European world. Then he conquered it for his use in his *Universal Empire*.

The 19th century took the romantic revolution and made it into the scientific revolution. A pudgy little Jewish man who hated rich people named Karl Marx, working with a dour Malthusian disciple named Friedrich Engels, came up with a theoretical description of Anglo-European Society that was elegantly verifiable by all the data of experience. They called it *dialectical materialism*. It set at naught anything romantic, emotional, spiritual, or even personal. Their religion was historical inevitability. Their god was revolution. Their heaven was a classless, stateless society that they called *communism*.

In our journey through the Eras, Levels, and Activities of the world, we have learned, have we not, that the Preacher, Ecclesiastes, was right when he said, "Know ye not that there is no new thing on the face of the earth?" Everything in Marxism and then Leninism, Stalinism, Maoism, socialism, National Socialism, fascism, communism, even communitarianism, and every other "ism" and "ology" are all marriages of scientific and philosophical methods *without spirituality*. They all try to save humanity and they end up destroying humanity. They are inhuman in the way they hyper intellectualize and psychoanalyze people.

What do we conclude about the human level of government? From the Renaissance to the New Age, we are all striving to understand what it is to be human. We know that we are animals, but we know that we're not just animals. What is it exactly beyond the animal level that we are?

Religious humanism takes a "leap of faith" and says that human beings are some sort of a replica of God. The human being is a person capable of choosing righteousness and goodness. The human being can be taught absolute values. For the religious humanist, these values can be intuited and taught by personal example. The best human development takes place in families. Religious humanism went well in the American Revolution.

Radical secular humanism, as a direct descendant of the Age of Reason, never relies on faith or hope. It has no respect for the unobservable or the felt. Radical secular humanism inculcates values by conditioning behavior in a process of rational socialization. For the radical secular humanist, social norms are best imparted by sound theoretical training. Radical secular humanism went badly in the French Revolution.

Good government at the human level grants individual judgment, choice, and freedom of action. Humane government honors natural (inalienable) rights derived from natural law. These lead to human rights and civil rights.

Human level government holds government accountable to the people and to whatever serves as the accepted, legitimate, national structure. Hopefully, this is a constitution. To put it another way, humane government rules by consent of the governed.

John Stuart Mill was a leading political theorist for the new Liberal Party in Britain and, in 1859, wrote an Essay entitled *On Liberty* wherein he says, "Every right has a concomitant duty." This means that the people give reasoned obedience to the rule of law.

It seems that human history is a succession of "big ideas" and that the big idea of our time is democracy. Democracy with its Anglo-American-European forms of voting, elections, civilian government, free press, independent judiciary, and the federal principle is irresistible by Party Chairmen, Supreme Leaders, and Presidents for Life. This is fine as long as we remember to govern democracy with a *constitution* that guarantees *rights*. Democracy without a constitution is "mobocracy" by factions.

Human level government sounds good and it is good, but it is frail. Constitutional democracy can degenerate into dictatorship and totalitarianism if the people do not have *spiritual level education*.

Adolf Hitler was freely and fairly elected Chancellor of Germany in 1932, whereupon he completely abrogated the Constitution of the Weimar Republic.

Patrick Henry said, "Bad men cannot make good citizens. It is when a people forget God that tyrants forge their chains. A vitiated state of morals, a corrupted public conscience is incompatible with freedom. No free government, or the blessings of liberty, can be preserved to any people but by a firm adherence to justice, moderation, temperance, frugality, and virtue; and by a frequent recurrence to fundamental principles."

Thus it is, that a spiritually educated people faces the last days before a turning of the cycle with a spiritual government.

SPIRITUAL LEVEL OF GOVERNMENT

Confucian ethics (which, we recall, began as advice to Kings on good government) are all about family and community obligations. According to Confucius, there is a natural order to life on earth which is, to be sure, logical and reasonable, but which is, more importantly, in *harmony* with the *spirit* of the Celestial Empire. To live and to rule in accordance with this harmony is to have the *Mandate of Heaven*. To live and to rule in violation of this harmony is to lose the Mandate of Heaven.

Confucius was a philosopher for hire and a consultant. He went from king to king peddling his perfect, ethical state. In his lifetime, nobody was buying. The human level is very hard to attain and maintain, let alone the spiritual level.

In the west, people who actually participated in government and also scholars of political philosophy worked on models of the perfect state. They used the Greek term *Utopia* for their creation, meaning "no place." Thus, they acknowledged this Platonic form of the perfect state did not exist…yet.

In France, Britain, and America, *communities* (religious and secular) were formed that tried to act out, if only on a small scale, a social order that was harmonious, humane, happy, prosperous, and secure. Most achieved some, but not all of these worthy goals.

"Christ, not man, is king," said Oliver Cromwell. Christ is a king, but he rules with love. He never compels. What would be a spiritual kingdom ruled over by Christ or, if we prefer, by God?

What are the features of a spiritual level government? It is no government at all. That is, it is an invisible government, because it governs the actions of human beings as the physical laws of nature (and nature's God) govern the movement of the planets and stars of the universe. It is an act of faith in spiritual education and spiritual government to teach people correct principles and then let them govern themselves.

In *The Book of Genesis*, in Paul's *Epistle to the Hebrews*, and in *the Epistle of Jude* there is reference to the prophet, Enoch. There is also an apocryphal *Book of Enoch* used by Muslims, Jews, and Christians. These all tell how Enoch led a people who created a righteous community of love called the "City of Zion" where everybody was "pure in heart." This book says that Enoch and the City of Zion were so righteous, so without conflict or unhappiness, that they did not die. They were "translated"…carried up into heaven, city and all, "without tasting of death." This is a spiritual level government.

I conclude that a spiritual level government is a community of people who are trying to be, as all my spiritual influences taught, enlightened to the point of being one with God.

The social and political movement known as *anarchism* (Greek: no ruler or no order) says that their definition of anarchy is "perfect freedom." Thomas Hobbes reminds us that indulgent, selfish, animal level people would make anarchy not perfect freedom, but perfect tyranny. Obedience to God (whom *the Bible* says is logos – logic, reason, order) is perfect freedom.

Can spiritual level government exist in this world? Not so far. After all, *we are only human*. Small instances are known in a time of great need (natural disaster, resistance to tyranny, outpouring of sympathy for a national or international tragic loss). Since the need will only get greater, let us unite in a *Worldwide Crusade for Biorelativity* that will lift us to a truly spiritual level of self government.

Where *none* are in control the principle of spiritual problem solving has prevailed. The more civilized man becomes the more problems will be prevented through the combined efforts of a majority or all the people. The ultimate goal in government and life is not to even think in terms of "problems." Man will eventually reach a point where he will be so overwhelmingly engaged in the processes of creation (almost by "miracle") that he will be in perfect harmony with all the laws and forces of life. This will be the Spiritual Age when *all* people will be in control of the government.

No limitations? What a marvelous, *dynamic* statement about human beings. We have no limitations except those which we place on ourselves. *We do it to ourselves.* The devil did *not* make us do it. Man, through his gift of free will from God, has done it to himself. Surely mankind is beginning to get awake. Man is truly a super being and does not know it, but awakening has begun.

Nations of the world are badly in need of some kind of carefully planned procedure for crossing the *critical line* to the spiritual level. This is so daunting when we struggle just to achieve the human level.

Once a human or majority rule level of government is set up, then some means is needed to help those nations maintain stability in their tender years of self-rule, which the Greeks named democracy. The majority rule – human level must arrive and stabilize upon a firm foundation of a human level in all the other activities of transportation, communication, education, occupations and other areas of culture and growth.

Nations around the globe are moving up to and across the critical line. Once across, even many industrialized nations bounce back and forth across this line in times of critical stress. It is extremely difficult for a people to be ruled hundreds of years by monarchy, oligarchy, aristocracy, or some revolutionary ideology and then suddenly be faced with the procedures of self rule by constitutional democracy.

One last thought on government. The ultimate step in government is to see ourselves both as planetary citizens and as universal citizens. The spirit (soul) is an eternal citizen of the universe. There is not one soul now on planet earth which was not also once somewhere else in space, in "the spirit world," and will someday be back with God again. That is the spiritual goal of God's government.

FIGURE 19

CHAPTER TWELVE
OCCUPATIONS

Jesus said, "The laborer is worthy of his hire." (1 Tim 5: 18)

Confucius said, "If you would govern a state of a thousand chariots, you must pay strict attention to business, be true to your word, be economical in expenditure and love the people." (*Analects*)

According to the *Book of Genesis* in the *Old Testament*, when Adam and Eve were cast out of the Garden of Eden, Adam was told, "In the sweat of thy face shalt thou eat bread."

In this dynamic world, there is a moral law as powerful as any physical law which says to all creatures on earth "As you sow, so shall you reap." There is a great lesson for mankind in the fall from innocence in the garden. Once we are born into mortality, then, along with all the other animals, we must get a living from the earth even as they do while we rise to a human and ultimately to a spiritual level of existence.

If this life is indeed a probationary state where we prove by our acts, thoughts, and choices that we are worthy to return to the presence of our Father in Heaven, then we must participate in the occupations of mankind here on the Earth.

The central factor used for the evaluation of occupations is the material with which the individual has experiences. There are five major levels of material in creation: mineral, plant, animal, human and spiritual. When one of these levels of material tends to dominate the environment and experiences of the individual, then it can be said that such is the name of the person's main level of occupation, even though some degree of all levels is present in every occupation.

MINERAL LEVEL OCCUPATIONS

These are the occupations of survival, wherein all life forms "live off the land." Plants get life from absorbing mineral soils as well as water borne minerals and life giving oxygen from the air. Animals graze on plants or hunt each other. Humans are hunter gatherer warriors, competing with everything else in the environment for food, clothing, and shelter.

PLANT LEVEL OF OCCUPATIONS

Now humans "live for the land." Humans make use of technology to control plants and animals, to use plants and animals to make human society. This is agriculture and animal husbandry. Building homes and tribal crafts are now possible.

ANIMAL LEVEL OF GOVERNMENT

Now humans "live on the land." Humans develop relationships with each other to make a group power that is equal to the power of the land. Building towns and organizing territories are now possible. There are occupations of culture, art, and religion.

HUMAN LEVEL OF GOVERNMENT

These are the occupations of human multiplying and subduing the Earth. Now humans can live above any considerations of the land. Humans replenish (or exploit) the Earth. Humans develop relationships with each other to make a group power that is superior to the power of the land. Humans can change the land.

SPIRITUAL LEVEL OF GOVERNMENT

These are the occupations of humans beyond Earthly concerns. Now humans can save the land and each other. Spirit sons and daughters of Heavenly Father and Heavenly Mother develop the power and authority to create heaven on earth.

Where there is growth, there is continual occupational change. The greater the growth, the greater is the change. The numbers in the figures below are estimates to show the patterns and proportions of dynamic change in occupations as one of the activities of man.

OCCUPATIONAL CHANGE

PAST	PRESENT	FUTURE
Medicine Man Slave Driver	Minister Teacher	Philosopher Psychologist
←———————— CRITICAL LINE ————————→		
Hunter Tree Dweller Stone Mason	Dairyman Gardener Miner	Zoologist Botanist Chemist

FIGURE 20

We have seen how occupations began with family, clan, and tribal division of labor. There was "men's work" which fathers taught by example to sons and "women's work" which mothers taught by example to daughters.

The men's work was the survival of the human family. Every man who would be a man was a hunter and a warrior. Every woman who would be a woman was a home-maker and a gatherer. Men were craftsmen of the clothing, equipment, tools and weapons of the men. Women crafted the tools and clothing of the home. Men brought the food to the women and the women made of the food a meal.

As human society became civilization, there was division of labor and what Marx identified as "classes" evolved into a complex and advanced social and economic organization. We passed through times of slavery and indentured or "bond" servants. We saw castes and callings. We were in craft guilds and merchant trades. We grew ever more and more professions. Secularization and freedom gave us (in the west at least) capitalism with its entrepreneurs.

As we advanced into the world of technical "magic," scientists and mathematicians became critical occupations. Artisans were not enough to make the things of modern human civilization. There had to be designers and engineers.

The rise of economic and political democracy required the occupations of communications for journalism, marketing, and a government's relations with its public.

Always there were the necessary decorators and adorners of buildings and people and true artists who didn't fit anywhere. They were deemed to be the expressers of the soul of their society and were patronized by royal or noble or political powers or they were deemed to be the judges of society and instigators of rebellion and were crushed or driven out by those same powers.

Artists and journalists are something like the priest professors of medieval universities or the priest playwrights of classic Greece. Artists and journalists preach the gospel of the human spirit and the humane attitude. In that way, they elevate all the people to remember that they are more than their occupations (which are still, after thousands of years, devoted to getting a living from the Earth). The people are members of an ever widening circle of family and community *because* of the messages received from works of art and from the journalistic art.

Over all occupations (though unacknowledged as such) were and are the educators. All occupations were gained by education and training. With the proliferation of occupations came a proliferation of educational and training venues. More and more, no occupation is possible without ever more advanced education.

Today we know that formal education and practical training are continuous throughout life. Every occupation has an initial qualification experience followed by a lifelong program of "career enrichment" and "professional development." In the human era and at the human level, ambition necessitates education. Education enables civilization. Leaders are trainers. Everybody is always a student. If you are not learning, you are not growing. If you are not growing, you cannot advance. If you do not advance, you will drop out. A feature of the advanced human era and level is competition. If you don't compete, you don't participate.

Parallel Growth. One of the main points to notice about occupations and education is the principle or trend of parallel growth. Education and occupations vary directly. That is, the level of occupations rises as the level of education rises. The one helps the other. They are interdependent and coexisting.

Gradually, this phenomenon will come to pass as man achieves automation and learns how to tap the sun's unlimited source of energy. Hour by hour the work-week will shorten, and the life- week will lengthen. Gradually, parents will have the time, the money, and the education to do a continuously better job with the education of their children whom they have created biologically as well as socially.

Occupations and Leisure Time. If man continues to live longer and work less, what will that do to his leisure time? That is another question which is largely answered before it is asked. The "miracle" just described above, of more mental life and less muscle work, can only be accomplished by the use of more intelligence and spiritual enlightenment.

One of the greatest fallacies of the last one hundred years is the belief that the thirty hours which were taken from the work week were wasted time because they were turned into leisure time. Now we don't call it leisure time, but rather *personal* time for "personal enrichment." Time nurturing self or family is not wasted. It is considered to be an investment in spiritual and intellectual stimulation influencing all behavior, public and private, and increasing the productivity of all occupations.

This, at least, is our image of the climax of the Human Era. We haven't yet really broken with the mineral-plant-animal past. The *whole child* is no more developed in our schools and social institutions than the whole power of our fuels is released in our *fire-burning* motors. Man today knows that the earth is round, but he is just getting awake to the fact that it is also *dynamic.*

The general trend of occupations in a healthy society is toward the creation of more human level jobs than are closed by science and progress. Science and progress create whole new industries and whole new occupations. This is particularly illustrated by the so-called "green" industries and technologies that have responded to our planetary environmental crisis. Another part of this trend is the proliferation of automation. Automation is not to be feared, because it requires whole new industries like robotics.

As man becomes more civilized, the lower level of jobs which are not discarded completely will become more automated. For every job or activity that is closed by automation below the critical line, there will be many more new jobs opened above the critical line. This is another way of saying that the more that is learned about being, the more occupational opportunities there are in this dynamic world.

OCCUPATIONS FOR ALL

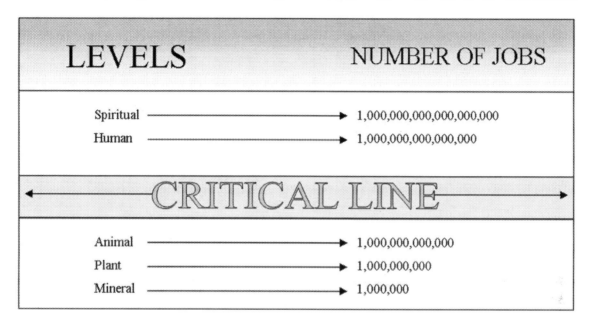

LEVELS		NUMBER OF JOBS
Spiritual	→	1,000,000,000,000,000,000
Human	→	1,000,000,000,000,000
CRITICAL LINE		
Animal	→	1,000,000,000,000
Plant	→	1,000,000,000
Mineral	→	1,000,000

FIGURE 21

Jobs are like knowledge in a dynamic world. The more one creates, the more there are to create. Therefore, pure leisure time is an illusion.

Obviously, this flowering of occupations in sync with education and this economic creativity of new industries is spread over the world very unevenly. Division of labor must now be organized globally.

For example, the so-called developed world (the west) has sent all, most, or much of its heavy industry to the so-called underdeveloped world that can produce major end items cheaper and better. This has caused painful dislocation in the developed world, but the adjustment to service, light industry, and creation of intellectual property has ended up advancing the developed world still farther ahead. The developed world dominates the information age more than ever. Hardware comes from Asia. Software (where the real money is and where the real education goes) is in America.

Thus, within the evolving structure of creative human activity there will develop a philosophy of life which does not reckon time by means of such negative terms as work. However, this way of life will result in an end product which is many times more effective than traditional work activities. Man's ability to work, augmented by science and automation, will be so productive that when he seems to be doing nothing, he will actually be performing miracles.

PERCENTAGES OF CREATION & CONSUMPTION

% LEVELS OF CREATION	% LEVELS OF CONSUMPTION
Spiritual 100	Mineral 0
Human 75	Plant 25

⟵ CRITICAL LINE ⟶

Animal 50	Animal 50
Plant 25	Human 75
Mineral 0	Spiritual 100

FIGURE 22

Remember creation and consumption? This figure shows how creation to consumption ratios are influenced for good by increasingly intelligent production.

The chief occupation of man in the future will be the improvement of his mind and his body. What man needs to do to make the great transition to the spiritual level, is cleanse and control the mind and body which now entrap the spirit. The body is the temple of the soul, and if man does not stop harming this temple "which ye are," God will destroy us. (I Corinthians 3:11-12)

OCCUPATIONS & HEALTH

OCCUPATIONAL LEVEL	FOOD LEVEL (cosmic energy)
Spiritual	Mineral
Human	Plant

←———————— CRITICAL LINE ————————→

Animal	Animal
Plant	Human
Mineral	Spiritual

FIGURE 23

We destroy ourselves with the "five whites" of refined (aka simple) carbohydrate – white sugar, white flour, white potato, white oil, and white fat (shortening, lard, etc.). We destroy ourselves with the distilled essence of those five white refined carbohydrates – food alcohol. We destroy ourselves with tobacco, abuse of drugs (legal and illegal), sexual immorality and excess, and a thousand other addictions.

Negative activities or occupations do destroy the body. Man is committing suicide in these ways. I knew a fellow who would eat twelve hot dogs per meal. He died at age 47. He committed hot dog suicide. How about diet coke suicide? How about 60% obesity in the United States? Education and elevating the level of occupations in a more humane economy makes for a population that understands health. Health care is the largest industry in the United States today. Movement of occupations toward the spiritual level will make the wellness industry the largest industry in the U.S.

Occupations and Food. What you eat can shorten or lengthen your life. The higher the level of occupation, the lower the level of material consumed for food. Yes, I am basically a vegetarian, but what comes next? Eating limestone? Well, almost. I take some calcium tablets and eat the minerals which are in plants.

OCCUPATIONS & POPULATION

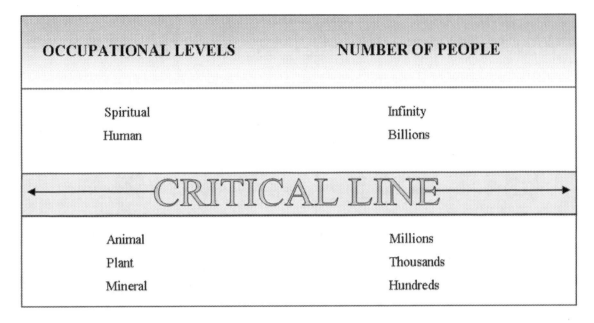

OCCUPATIONAL LEVELS	NUMBER OF PEOPLE
Spiritual	Infinity
Human	Billions
←————— CRITICAL LINE —————→	
Animal	Millions
Plant	Thousands
Mineral	Hundreds

FIGURE 24

The higher the level of occupation and life, the more an increase in the number of high level people is needed. Progress requires people *in a higher level of consciousness.* Currently, we have overpopulation of lower consciousness people who hurt rather than heal the total environment. We are not Malthusians. We do not say, with Scrooge in *The Christmas Carol,* "Let them die, then, and decrease the surplus population." We say, let them rise, then, and increase an abundance of creation. Let people not fight over smaller and smaller pieces of the "pie," but rather work together to make a *bigger pie!* Spiritual people think abundance, not scarcity.

OCCUPATIONS & COMPENSATION

LEVELS	CREATIVE PAY	DOLLAR PAY
Spiritual	1,000,000,000,000	0
Human	1,000,000	100

◄────── CRITICAL LINE ──────►

Animal	1,000	1,000
Plant	100	10,000
Mineral	1	1,000,000

FIGURE 25

Notice that creative pay and consumptive or dollar pay vary inversely. Second, see that the highest dollar pay is with the lowest level of environment.

One of the most outstanding things about creative or spiritual pay is the fact that it tends to come during the working activity. The higher the level of the working environment, the higher is the level of creative pay. Creative pay tends to prevent sickness and diseases. The greater the creative pay the less the dollar pay needed to go with it.

At the highest level of creative pay, the spiritual level, the individual might even be getting zero dollars to go with it. This is generally known as the virtue of non-attachment or renunciation. It has also been called the Law of Consecration. Or as Jesus would say, sell your riches and material possessions and give them to the poor, take up your cross and follow me.

Each person must decide what combination of environmental factors he/she is willing to endure during the current lifetime.

At the spiritual level of occupation, people do not find a job; they pray to know their personal vocation (calling). Your calling in life is that creative occupation for which you were born, for which God gave you your talents and gifts.

The world is poised for the Great Transition to a new spiritual era! What is the role of spiritual people in bringing all brothers and sisters over the line? Teach them the great news of all that is coming. Show them all that is there for them. *CRUSADE FOR BIORELATIVITY!*

CHAPTER THIRTEEN
COMMUNICATIONS

MINERAL LEVEL OF CREATIVE COMMUNICATION

At the mineral level, communication is literal and immediate. That is to say, communication is pre-symbolic. It is not figurative. It is concrete and not abstract. Communication is either the phonetic code of language or a non-language code of visual, physical, or vocal messages. Mineral level communication is "body language," touch language, and verbal language of present tense instructions, past tense reports, and future tense intentions or predictions.

PLANT LEVEL OF CREATIVE COMMUNICATION

At the plant level, a sentient being, man or mollusk, can respond to the stimulation of the environment and convey the quality of that response to fellows. An advanced animal, like a wolf, can howl at the moon and a man (even a Cro-Magnon one) can gasp with wonder or terror. This communication can create relationships and plans of action. This communication can signal the most primitive emotion. Communication can create an ambience that affects everything in the ambient area.

ANIMAL LEVEL OF CREATIVE COMMUNICATION

At the animal level, communication is emotional and all about relationships. Animals, like plants, are aware of the quality of vibrations being communicated through the ether. We once had a dog which became very angry every time a certain person came to visit us. That person seemed so nice when talking to us, but the communication to our dog was not good. There was a subconscious mind conditioning in that person's mind which was being communicated to the dog. You might call this a kind of sixth sense ability. Animal level communication reads aural vibrations. Specifically, animals can form relationships with and understand non symbolic messages from humans.

HUMAN LEVEL OF CREATIVE COMMUNICATION

The human level of creative communication is composed of everything available in the previous levels and then adds self consciousness as well as symbolic or figurative communication. Human communication, verbal or non-verbal, can communicate – to a human who knows the code of language -- *abstractions*. Human level communication uses symbolic language, figurative language, and elliptical or indirect language to put across extremely complex descriptions of reality to include internal reality. Additionally, human level communication can be in a written or electronic code. Human communication can be in visual images or non-verbal sounds (for example, music).

The problem with the human level of anything is that humans, with enormous intelligence but without wisdom, advance themselves to God-like levels of capability with ungodly results.

In the 1991 First Edition of *This Dynamic World*, I wrote:

'The Thinking Machine.' Now, here is a problem. What is human level thinking and communicating is so able, so skillful, that human beings can create a thinking machine, an artificial intelligence. Of course, they have done this. It is the computer.

'The Thinking Machine' is the title of an article in a digest of essays about this problem entitled *The Computerized Society*, edited by Edward Cornish, and published by World Future Society, Bethesda, Maryland, 1985. Mr. Cornish explains the dilemma which evolves as mankind today takes consumptive communication and arrives at a level of communication creativity which can be the undoing of mankind, because the human creator seems to lack the higher level of morality needed to give the machine ethics and morals. It is a machine. It can not judge situations spiritually because it has no soul. Without a positive essence or spirit, *great communication becomes great destruction.*

Quoting from 'The Thinking Machine:'

Lewis Branscomb, IBM's vice president for research, has projected that a computer in the twentieth century may have the power of 16,000 human brains—and even that awesome projection could fall short of future reality. Biochips could also hasten the day when human brains are physically linked together, thereby creating a new race of superintelligent cyborgs. Possibly there will be a way to hook our brains into a computer so that we acquire its memory. This man-machine symbiosis might lead to an entirely new form of human experience and a tremendous increase in human capabilities.

Already, experiments are under way to use computers and robots to replace the functions of defective body organs. Paraplegics, for instance, may use voice commands to direct robots that can prepare a meal, remove a tray, or provide a drink. . . . People will find it increasingly easy to speak to computers in ordinary language and ask them to solve the most abstruse scholarly or mathematical problem. The computer's awesome capabilities may both thrill and frighten us. If computers can do so much, will there be any need for people in the future? Is the computer a humble and faithful servant or a new God? (Is it) a loyal friend and worthy colleague, or an evil force that is now devouring our humanity like an electronic cancer." p. 5

The thinking machine cannot be used to conquer your neighbor. The thinking machine must only be used for the holistic support of human, spirit to spirit communications.

If these computers and thinking machines are so great, surely they can be used to unify mankind into one planetary citizenship. If our current round of "religious wars" cannot be stopped, mankind will be destroyed. The thinking machines must be enlisted on the side of humanity itself.

So I wrote at the dawn of the Information Age. This was when we first faced cyber war in cyber space, cyber terror, cyber robbery (or, if you prefer, information "highway robbery"), hacking, blogging, internet marketing, internet journalism, chat rooms, cyber predators and cyber rape resulting in very real death, messaging, pop up porno, dating services, prostitution services (one masquerading as the other), internet gambling or (indistinguishable) investing, youtube, facebook, and twitter.

Now the simple electronic window of television is thinking too with streaming video, DVR, SKYPE, and TiVO.

Even so, this is not of itself "bad." The dangerous element comes from the use of all these thinking machines for evil purposes -- selfishness, hate, revenge, money, etc. And not even this would be impossible to deal with except that man on earth speaks through 4,000 different languages, 159 nations, nine major religions, and then huge numbers of people in each nation which are illiterate. This is a nightmare of misinterpretations. So we end up imploding economies in cyber depressions of financial chaos, fighting wars and killing millions of people and destroying trillions of dollars of resources purely because of misunderstandings over the interpretation of words.

The earth's cyber community becomes saturated with a cloud of electronic pollution which is totally unnecessary.

When this point is reached the obvious solution is a World Wide (Cyber) Crusade of Biorelativity. . So mankind is faced with a choice: clean up, or shut up. We must either clean up the "mind field" around the earth, or an inharmonic network will trigger major conflicts, anomalies, electromagnetic pulses and earth changes, such as earthquakes, which will *make* us shut up.

SPIRITUAL LEVEL OF CREATIVE COMMUNICATION

Far superior to the human level of communication and far harder to attain is the spiritual level of communication, sometimes called "know by knowing." The *super conscious* mind has *omnipresence* and can read *universal mind*. All spiritual traditions say that this is what God does. We have learned from all my sources that transcendent meditation to the point of enlightenment and power can communicate calls to action, calls for help, calls for blessings, and calls for warning. This community praying, meditating, and exhorting for all good things inspires spiritual people to take action. It also increases the spirituality of those prayed for to become spiritual so they hear the call and have a new found desire to take action. Christians would call this repentance and conversion. This is the central principle of the Worldwide Crusade for Biorelativity.

A New Age way to put it goes like this. Humans have a soul. The level of soul-awareness which a human being has determines the amount of communication which can be received from the all knowing Universal Mind. At the soul level, humans know what God knows. This puts a human being in touch with higher dimensions of vibrations. People like Jeanne Dixon can read a communication from both past events recorded in Universal Mind, as well as things which will happen in the future. This is the spiritual level of communication which can be developed by anyone through meditation and *looking within*, as the New Age people say.

The Paramahansa Yogananda would say that God speaks to us through the Soul, if only we know how to listen. With desire, patience, determination, will power and the practice of meditation, we can improve our knowing via the soul. The Soul knows what God knows, if only we can become soul aware. Every thought enters Universal Mind, thus God knows all. A positive thought for world peace vibrates or is communicated around the globe and sends a harmonic message to all people and living things, all beings of space, as well as the living entity of the earth itself. Praying is talking with God, which anyone can do, but the higher the level of consciousness the more effective or the better the communication of the prayer. Each prayer raises the level of consciousness some. You don't have to be a preacher to pray, but if you pray enough you will become a preacher.

Universal Magnetism and Communication. There is a system of communication which pervades the universe; all parts communicating with all parts. This great method of communication is a system known as *Universal Mind.* It seems to have something to do with at least a metaphorical (and possibly literal) *magnetism.* We say, "I am attracted to" a person, an idea, or a state of being or we say, "I am repelled by" a person, an idea, a state of being. We also describe a "magnetic personality."

There is an analog to New Age spirituality (or religion) called *New Thought*, which delves into the power of this spirit to spirit communication. In her book, *The Secret*, Rhonda Byrne describes *The Law of Attraction.* The concept of the Law of Attraction is that you must…

> ➢ Know exactly what you want.
> ➢ Ask the universe (God) for it.
> ➢ Know that the object of your desire is already yours.
> ➢ Visualize the moment of your success.
> ➢ Behave as if you have attained your objective.
> ➢ Be open to receive it and let go of your attachment to the outcome.

Byrne's "secret," then, is that, "Thinking of what one does not have, they (New Thought proponents) say, manifests itself in not having, while, if one abides by these principles and avoids negative thoughts, the universe will manifest a person's desires."

This Law of Attraction is, I believe, a re-statement of the older and well accepted *Power of Positive Thinking* by Norman Vincent Peale (Prentice-Hall. 1952, 1956, 1983). All my sources would agree that positive thinking and a positive attitude positively make things happen in accordance with *positive affirmations.*

The Hindu yogis call it Karma (fate, destiny, predestination, but caused by "self-fulfilling prophecy"). As the Hindu treatise, *Dhammagada*, says:

Mind is the master power that moulds and makes,
And man is mind, and evermore he takes
The tool of thought, and, shaping what he wills,
Brings forth a thousand joys, a thousand ills:—
He thinks in secret, and it comes to pass:
Environment is but his looking-glass.

Good King Solomon put it very simply in *Proverbs* 23:7. "As a man thinketh in his heart, so is he."

Thus, spiritual communication sent as a group message or sent by an individual to another individual or manifesting an internal monologue of a person within him or herself *accesses the power of the universe* which is, as we have heard our sources say, the mind of God (or universal mind). This is superconsciousnesstothepointof*cosmicconsciousness*.Itpervadeseveryareaoflifeandeverypartofevery sentient being. This is Paul's "faith that removes mountains" (in 1 Corinthians 13). This is power that will save your life and save your world.

Spirit to spirit communications – aided or impeded by thinking machines – make us all *planetary citizens* in this dynamic world.

CHAPTER FOURTEEN
RELIGION

Religion is an activity that must be human. Animals can be spiritual. They can experience wonder and awe. Animals can love and mourn and sacrifice. But animals cannot inquire. They cannot make use of all the intellectual, emotional, and spiritual processes implicit in *logos*. Animals cannot analyze and synthesize. They cannot do symbolic things. All this is necessary to understand God. We do it because we are spirit sons and daughters of God.

Of course, primitive man engaged in primitive religion tied to primeval things like the relationship with earth, sky, sun, plants, and animals. All these things and more have been personified and deified.

Let us now use our system of study to work through the levels of religion. We orient once again to the levels through which mankind has to rise. As always this establishes the trend we follow and the critical line over which we must cross on our way to the highest (spiritual) level.

MINERAL LEVEL OF RELIGION

The mineral level of religion is the first and lowest level. By mineral level religion, we mean the impulse of human beings living at the mineral level to explain how their environment works with mystical and spirit ways rather than scientific and mathematical ways.

Mineral level people tend to be *animists*. Animism is an anthropological term meaning the belief that every life form and, indeed, every inanimate object has a spirit. This spirit is a sentient being that controls its particular part of the environment. Human beings then and human beings now want to *personify* animals, plants, and the forces of nature.

Ancient Japanese religion says that every object as well as every organism has a *kami* or spirit. Many cultures worshipped the sun as a god, including high, sophisticated cultures purporting to be spiritual. Mineral level people describe the workings of nature in personified metaphorical ways. For example, there are plenty of cultures that worship Father Sun and Mother Earth. In our western culture, the most famous example of mineral level religion is the paganism of Greece and Rome. Here, not only is every part of the environment and every force of nature personified as a very human appearing god or goddess, but so is every human virtue, vice, or activity.

PLANT LEVEL OF RELIGION

The plant level of religion is the second level. This level of religion parallels the agricultural level of humanity. Many early agricultural people worship a plant god, such as a Native American corn god or an Asian rice god. Desiring control over the agricultural process and the weather it depended on, plant level people worship a god for each part of the process. There is a god of rain and the demon of drought. There is much comparing of human fertility to fertility of the land. In many cultures, there is a great concern for the winter and summer solstice. When, during the winter, father sun is going away, there are all kinds of rites and sacrifices to beg him to not abandon the earth. When the summer solstice comes, there is great rejoicing and more rites and sacrifices of gratitude.

We are making mineral and plant level religions seem childish and weak minded. Anyone who has dealt humbly with devoted practitioners of these religions knows that there is a profound spirituality in connecting with these cosmic forces, which, after all, are mastered by God.

But modern agriculture has generally dethroned the corn god.Not so the indirect plant god. Millions of people have become addicted to drugs from plants, such as marijuana, cocaine and tobacco nicotine. Some individuals sacrifice their jobs to the drug god. Others give up their family, their homes, and even their health. Tobacco related illnesses kill some 350,000 Americans per year. They die for their "plant gods."

ANIMAL LEVEL OF RELIGION

We have seen that pagans worshipped gods and goddesses with human traits. They were also in awe of human like relationships between gods, goddesses, and humans. There is powerful and profound dramatization of real human character and personality in the stories of the gods. These stories instruct profound truths. They are their parables.

HUMAN LEVEL OF RELIGION

The human level of religion is the fourth level. This is a level where advanced, sophisticated human societies have been taught about the true and living god. They have been taught about creation, salvation, ordinances and sacraments. Such people are trying to do the right thing and they are honoring beautiful principles that have been taught to their ancestors. Alas, they are actually worshipping human achievement. They worship the human spirit and human community even though they truly believe they are worshipping God.

Here we run into a subtle but critical disagreement among believers. There are many people in all of the great religions of the world who believe in the fatherhood of god, the brotherhood of man, and the family of man. That is to say, such people insist that all humans are spirit sons and daughters of Heavenly Father and Heavenly Mother. They would insist that this is not some sort of self serving, self justifying "human" need, but rather honest, spiritual level, true religion.

No one should dismiss the heavenly family model of godhead without considering the spiritual impact that belief has on the fundamental human relationship, which is, of course, the family.

The greatest social problem of man today the world over is disintegration of the family. There are many who argue that wrong headed views of marriage and family spring not only from radical secular humanism, but also from a belief that a "first family of heaven" from which we all came and to which we all wish to return is somehow weakly human and not the ultimate spirituality. The body less, impersonal god of pure mind, on the other hand, is somehow so unknowable as to not be useful in the daily fight against the extremely knowable and extremely understandable Satan.

At any rate, human level religion is what we see out in the world today. It is either an honest and honorable attempt to find God and do his will for the good that will bring *or* it is a dishonest and dishonorable attempt to please society and protect oneself with the armor of appropriateness.

SPIRITUAL LEVEL OF RELIGION

The spiritual level of religion is, of course, the highest level. This is the level of actual contact with God through spirit to spirit communication. We can study thousands of pages of thousands of works of theology and philosophy by thousands of individuals over thousands of years in thousands of cultures. We can get great human wisdom, insight, and benefit of experience from all this human effort. But what we want is to know the truth. So we glean from this great human record the little pearls of great price where people can convince us that they actually communicated with God, even walked and talked with God.

Throughout my account of this dynamic world, I have respectfully acknowledged sincere attempts at spirituality by spiritual leaders in all faiths and cultures and ages. I have also recounted my personal evolution to my own convictions. God, I believe, is a master soul with a mind that runs the entire universe of which our souls and our minds are tiny parts. I do not say insignificant parts. Each one of us has within us the power of God to rule over the universe. Together, I believe, we can actually make our planet and our part of universe be what we will it to be. God, I believe, has sent us avatars, sons of God, messengers of God, to teach us what we ought to do with our world.

I observe that all of the world's religions (represented by their avatars) teach us essentially the same things. They teach us that…

- ➤ God is love.
- ➤ We are love and must love one another.
- ➤ We must have faith in the reality of God's (and our) power.
- ➤ We cannot just meditate and pray. We must act – in the name of God.
- ➤ We cannot just hope; we must help.

Part of the power of positive thinking is the power of faith. The apostle Paul said "Now faith is the substance of things hoped for, the evidence of things not seen…through faith we understand that the worlds were framed by the word of God, so that things which are seen were not made of things which do appear." (Hebrews 11:1-3) Seeing is believing, but believing can make possible a new way of seeing.

Modern humans proceed materialistically to try to achieve this immaterial understanding. They reason out how to build "time machines" and do "time travel." People with the kind of faith I have described know that you must progress (over time) to the *spiritual* level of *spiritual* experience with the things of God in order to comprehend let alone achieve a truly timeless state.

We can reach a spiritual level of being called by some a "God-like" state and by others an "astral" state on an astral plain of existence. We would then "see" the space-time continuum. We would pierce the illusion of time and space and connect with all times and all places. This is what Yogananda did with his Kriya Yoga. This is what Moses did on the mountain in Sinai. We would then be in "heaven" even if we find out that Heaven is on Earth.

This is where we all want to be, but how do we get there? We have learned about meditation, trances, media, communication and power through prayer, revelation, but all of these things are personal. They could even be called selfish. I want to know for the good it would do me. I want the power for the things I can do for myself. The ultimate paradox is that to get to Heaven, to pass through seven lives and on to Nirvana, to attain Enlightenment, we cannot think of ourselves. We must think about other people. We serve. We sacrifice ourselves and – like Job -- discover that we have attained twice as much as we sacrificed. We love. We bless. We help. We take care of.

Christians, for example, remember that (in Matthew 16:25) Christ said "Whosoever will save his life shall lose it and whosoever will lose his life for my sake shall find it." They remember what I called Christ's statement of the Tao. "I am the way, the truth, and the light." We must try our best to be Christ like. We must rise to the level of receiving personal revelation by committing to the spiritual way of life. How do we do that?

We must live true religion. What is that?

Pure religion and undefiled before God and the Father is this, to visit the fatherless and widows in their affliction and to keep himself (oneself) unspotted from the world." (James 1:27)

The Apostle Paul taught true or pure religion in his first letter to the Corinthians when he wrote,

> Though I speak with the tongues of men and of angels and have not charity, I am become as sounding brass or a tinkling cymbal. And though I have the gift of prophecy and understand all mysteries and all knowledge and though I have all faith so that I could remove mountains and have not charity, I am nothing. And though I bestow all my goods to feed the poor and though I give my body to be burned and have not charity, it profiteth me nothing. Charity suffereth long and is kind; charity envieth not; charity vaunteth not itself, is not puffed up, doth not behave itself unseemly, seeketh not her own, is not easily provoked, thinketh no evil, rejoiceth not in iniquity, but rejoiceth in the truth; beareth all things, believeth all things, hopeth all things, endureth all things.

Paul then addresses the issue of arriving at the Spiritual Era by rising to a spiritual level of existence where there is no concern for time.

> Charity never faileth: but whether there be prophecies, they shall fail; *whether there be times, they shall cease;* whether there be knowledge, it shall vanish away. For we know in part and we prophesy in part, but when that which is perfect is come, then *that which is in part shall be done away.* When I was a child, I spake as a child, I understood as a child, I thought as a child, but when I became a man, I put away childish things. For now *we see through a glass darkly, but then face to face.* Now I know in part, but then shall I know even as also I am known. And now abideth faith, hope, charity, these three, but the greatest of these is charity (1 Corinthians 13).

The way to advance from a materialistic, self centered age into a spiritual age is to serve people. Caring for people (Latin: caritas. English translation: charity) will teach us how to have what Christians call the Holy Spirit as our companion and comforter. The Holy Spirit will help us understand the space time continuum and its fabric.

In his revelation on the Isle of Patmos, John says that he saw

> ...a new heaven and a new earth: for the first heaven and the first earth were passed away; and there was no more sea... and God shall wipe away all tears from their eyes; and there shall be no more death, neither sorrow, nor crying, neither shall

there be any more pain: for the former things are passed away. (Rev 21:1-4)

But John also says that, while people shall be saved from death by the atonement of Jesus Christ, in order for them to enter into this spiritual state, they must have done the things that spiritual people do. Jesus said, "A new commandment I give unto you, that ye love one another; as I have loved you, that ye also love one another. (John 13:34) Every secular thing we do with social structure, social justice, society, and community comes from this commandment.

Paramahansa Yogananda says that we must master ourselves and teach each other how to be happy by connecting with the power of God. There is a discipline, a series of attainments, which will accomplish that. He taught me that we live in a sea of cosmic energy. If we can learn the right discipline, the right regimen, the right way of life, that energy will enter us and we will be happy. Shedding materialism puts us on an upward path toward this highest, spiritual level. It will make us happy to share what we know with others and we will bless each other. Everything we do today with "health food," "holistic health care," "wellness," and "anti-aging" come directly from the teachings and the inspiring examples of the Hindu yogis, frequently filtered through Aquarian New Age New Thought.

Albert Einstein, Steven Hawking, and the other quantum theorists could conceive of the space time continuum, but they could not enter the space time continuum. You can, if you will do all of the things spiritual leaders teach you to do to help other people. This is true enlightenment. This is the Way.

This is what prophets did and do to become prophets. This is how you get revelation. This is how you perform miracles. Do this and you will progress to a level of spirituality that approaches a God-like state *where there is no time*. Spiritual enlightenment can occur any time the individual decides to make it happen.

We have seen that observable science, calculable mathematics, revelations recorded in Scripture, and witness of personal experience --all explain this progression through eras. We know that the trend of all trends is mineral to plant to animal to human to God. We know that the critical line over which we humans want to step is the line between the material and the spiritual. Thanks to Einstein and Jesus, Hawking and Yogananda, Newton and Buddha, Rene Des Cartes and Confucius, we know how that works. Unfortunately, we also know that we cannot save ourselves. We have to save each other. We can never learn enough, or calculate enough, or build enough to carry ourselves over that line. We have to do something so difficult that Einstein never even thought of it much less attempted it. On the other hand, our task is so simple that a little child can lead us. Think about other people. Help other people. Love one another. Take care of the ones you love.

We cannot prevent the end of the world as ordained by God. However, it is the will of God that we do everything we can do to save the world. If we wish to be ready for the Second Coming or the Age of Aquarius or however we describe it, then we must do our duty to love one another and to love our mother the earth as God has loved us. Despite everything proclaimed by the Egyptians, the Mayans, the prophets -- ancient and modern -- and even Nostradamus, we cannot calculate the time of the end of the world. We must, however, heed the signs of the times and do what the Spirit tells us is right.

LEVELS
of
RELIGION

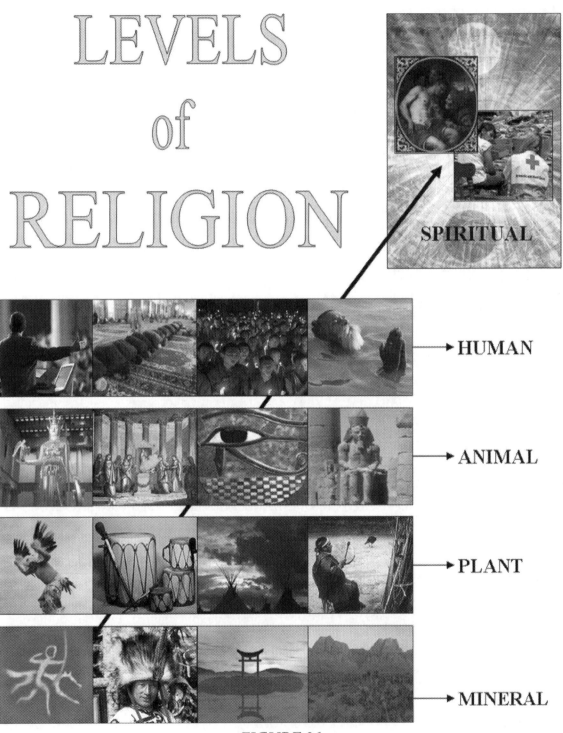

SPIRITUAL

HUMAN

ANIMAL

PLANT

MINERAL

FIGURE 26

CHAPTER FIFTEEN
THE WORLD WIDE CRUSADE OF BIORELATIVITY

SUMMA

I end as I began. Maybe just barely a little like Jesus of Nazareth, I came down from the hills, off my father's farm, and entered into the wide world which was full of trouble. Like young Mukunda Lal Ghosh, I ran away from home a little bit, but like Mukunda, I came back to my duty to become educated. Like Jesus, I discoursed with the "learned doctors." People said of Jesus, "Is this not the carpenter's son?" They said of me, "The hillbilly school teacher says what?" I went far away from home and saw war. In my life growing up and in my work as an educator of rough youth I dealt with deadly sins of addiction and ignorant selfishness.

I may be some kind of "Hindu preacher," though I never paid the price to be ordained as a yogi. I may, in my own way and as best I can, follow in the footsteps of visionary philosophers and formulate some sort of approach to saving the world that concretely explains to people what they should do. I certainly have not taken on the responsibility of government office.

I do feel powerfully impressed to proclaim a message for our time. I am certainly not a prophet and God has not called me to lead, but I cannot leave this life without a testament to the things I know are true and which I know are needed by all the world.

I have tried to pull together for you, from the history and learning of man and from the record of man's dealings with God, an explanation of the Christian Plan of Salvation and the Aquarian Plan of Happiness and an exhortation to you of what you can do to be saved and to help save the world.

I have tried to give my challenge to you a descriptive name that will excite you to a remembrance of great concepts. I call it a *World Wide Crusade of Biorelativity*. I hope my message and my challenge will go all over the world. To be effective, our effort must be worldwide. From 1095 to 1291, there were nine crusades for avowedly Christian purposes but frequently with behavior repugnant to Christ. Still, the word crusade has been used to good effect. A crusade is a spiritual and moral campaign to oppose some great evil and advance some great good. It is in that sense I call for holy crusade. Biorelativity is a term I have constructed to mean something parallel to Einstein's theory of relativity. So I mean a theory describing life as it passes through dynamic forces and changes that cause it to evolve in accordance with a plan or a theory.

You have considered what I laid out as the eras, levels, and activities of life within the space time continuum of the life of the universe. Here then is what we have to actually do to help the world over the critical line between the acceptable level and the necessary level.

WE DO IT TO OURSELVES

Jesus said, "Physician, heal thyself." Stop blaming outside forces for the bad things that happen. Ultimately, we do it to ourselves.

Sin. If you are a Christian, then you know that the first principle of the Gospel of Jesus Christ is faith – faith in the Lord, Jesus Christ. If you are convinced he is, in fact, the Christ, then you know that the next thing you must do is repent of your sins.

Everybody sins. Everybody is sinned against. All the negativity, defensiveness, even paranoia, the coveting, the lusting, the conspiring, the positioning, and the outright crimes in business, home, public life, private life … it's all just protecting your sins.

It's hard to give up your sins. They seem to be your only pleasures in life. The irony is, you're much happier and have a much more pleasant life if you give up the sins. Repent. Get rid of sin. Everything will go better. You will be much happier.

Addiction is the great Satan. So many sins are sins of addiction. Addiction is a bigger word than we think. It may be true that everybody is addicted to something. It is hard to take life straight. Whatever you call evil (Lucifer, Satan, Asuras of temptation, lying, and deceit) works on this. Satanic addiction craves an artificial ecstasy to ease a suffering that was caused by the craving in the first place. Satan says that you have a right to these things. They are a reward for your successful efforts. You are free. You should be liberated from all restrictions. Anarchy is perfect freedom, right?

The crushing irony is that these "rewards" do not free you. They enslave you. Anarchy is perfect tyranny. Yogananda sees past temptation to the joy of harmony, peace, and appreciation. Giri Bala learned that living on cosmic energy was much more pleasant than craving food. Jesus set the example in all things, including resisting temptation. He said to Satan, "Get thee behind me."

A SPIRITUAL ICE AGE

It seems to me that we are in a *spiritual ice age*. Everything fresh and lively and hopeful is frozen and dormant. We are ready for a "spring thaw" and a return of the sun that will be glorious. We are at the end of the Dark Age of Pisces and coming into the brilliant Age of Aquarius. We are working our way through the signs of the times of the last days before the end of the order of the world.

We can help the advance of the ages by nourishing and repairing ourselves and the world. In a temporal sense at least, we can save ourselves and save the world. In the end, there will be a final termination of the order we have built up over so many centuries, but we should act as though we were saving the world. We don't know when the end will come. Our efforts are not futile. And anyway, we show God our obedience to his commandments. He sees us doing the right thing.

In food, in building, in transportation, in health, in government, and in world clean up, we know what we have to do. It starts with our personal lives. You really do have control over your own life. In all the activities of human life, make good choices moment by moment.

Biotechnology or the science of life. By biotechnology, I mean all the environmentally sound technologies we have learned about in this dynamic world. From the neighborhood council to the Congress of the United States, be a good citizen. Be active. Contribute ideas. Agree to participate. Constantly add to your education in the science of diet, exercise, preventive health care, infrastructure, climate repair, living space, peaceful coexistence, sensible money management, and human relations. Visualize your heaven on earth and then work to make your little heavenly time and space. Help others. Cast your vote for the forces that will bless it rather than mess it up.

Yogaculture and cosmic energy. Not yogurt culture, although that's a good start. You are trying to fix your attention on ever more spiritual life. As you enjoy your body (in yoga, for instance), you are focusing on the sensual joy of how you feel and what you can do, not on how you can satiate your appetite. You are not denying your body nourishment and sustenance; you are just not obsessing about gratification.

Dark Age man will fixate on plants and animals to eat, and will always be hungry. Spiritual Age man will have the best of everything, But, "Seek ye *first* the kingdom of God and His righteousness, and all else (like a beautiful family and the way to give them every good thing) will be added unto you." If you drink of the well of Christ (cosmic energy?) you will have living water. Your real thirst and hunger will be quenched unto eternal life.

Here is a juicy tidbit you can chew on.

In *Food without Farming: The Biotech Revolution in Agriculture*, by Walter Truett Anderson, he says:

> Scientists can now take a slice from a leaf of a tree and put it into a medium of hormones and nutrients that cause it to grow into a callus, a mound of undifferentiated cells. A plant callus is not in itself a particularly inspiring sight— it looks a little like a helping of green mashed potatoes—but it has tremendous potential because every single cell in the callus has the genetic information to become a whole plant. In the proper medium the callus can produce a hundred— or a million copies of a single tree." (pp. 17-18) . . . The original source of whatever you may find on your dinner table is the sun.

Love learning. If learning is a passion for you, all physical joys will be more intense and more appreciated because you know what to value. Intelligence heightens happiness. Learn to feast on ideas. Ernest Hemingway called love of literature (his particular art) a "moveable feast." Luke says in his gospel account, "Feast upon the word of Christ." Education provides a spiritual feast. Instead of going through your day looking for that next "hit" (of sugar, dope, whatever), look for that next "natural high" of appreciation. That's how you live on cosmic energy.

Dispel the illusion of separateness. How can we get rid of this illusion of separateness? As I see it, we can only dissolve this illusion of separateness through love.

> ➢ love for the planet and all the environment
> ➢ love for all humans; and total love for God.

> ➤ Or we could do exactly what Jesus said in St. Mark 12:30, 31.

Thou shalt love the Lord thy God with all thy heart, and with all thy soul, and with all thy mind, and with all thy strength: this is the first commandment. And the second is like, namely this, Thou shalt love thy neighbor as thyself. There is none other commandment greater than these.

You will be happy if you will think of other people and help other people. You will be loved if you will love. The way you fall in love is to cherish your beloved. Service makes you feel good. Remember the Jewish doctor in the death camp. "To live is to suffer," he said. "To be happy is to find meaning in the suffering."

Energy release. Release the tensions that are trapping your energy. Relax. Think carefully. Decide. Act. Don't worry about it. Just do it.

Help the world release its energy in your highest and best service. Remember, the earth is a living organism the same as you are.

Here is a *mantra*:

Not fire… not water …solar, electromagnetic, wind, natural processes, fusion … energy of human creativity…human activity. Greenhouse gas is a negative example. Green house oxygenation is a positive example.

Charge your human body battery.

Live your spiritual religion. Pray as if everything depended on the Lord. Then act as if everything depended on you. Not to us, but to the Lord goes the glory.

"Now abideth these three, faith, hope, and charity, but the greatest of these is charity."

A DYNAMIC WORLD

If there is one final thought I would like to add, it is this. Have faith in the future. Be positive regardless of the day-to-day outlook about anything. Total failure is a condition that cannot happen to you no matter what evolves, because this is a great, dynamic world.

In a dynamic world, a positive attitude is your most basic requirement. All else is merely a part of the evolving process, up the ladder of life to greater conscious awareness. Even if death should befall you, and it will, don't worry. Continue to have faith in God in spite of death. For if you do, "death" then becomes a necessary cleansing process for your dynamic fulfillment in each future reincarnation or in future kingdoms in heaven.

Death, in the traditional viewpoint, is actually an illusion. There is no death for a soul, the real you. Death only comes to the body, the unreal you. The body is merely a coat, a covering, a vehicle for your convenience at a specific point in your continuous journey onward and upward.

So have faith in God. Be positive. Be happy. You cannot fail no matter what. Failure is also an illusion, for each problem is actually a lesson, a stepping stone, because you are a Child of God. Act like one. Think like one. Live like one. For you are one ... NOW!!

If there is any part of this book which you do not like, rewrite it; improve it. Every human being on earth (and beyond) is a coauthor.

I am 92 in human level years, but I certainly plan to keep on writing. There will be more practical suggestions on what we can do for this dynamic world. We are ready for action. The Cleansing Age has begun. Let us all THINK, PRAY and ACT our way into a peaceful, fulfilling, dynamic future together.

BIBLIOGRAPHY

In this Second Edition of *This Dynamic World*, I have added the wonders of the internet to the sources cited in my *Sources* section at the beginning of the work. I have made use of internet articles about those sources, particularly drawing upon *Wikipedia*, the internet encyclopedia. I have also made extensive use of periodicals such as *National Geographic*. I have also drawn upon general knowledge of such things as "The Renaissance," "Neo-Classicism," and so on. In such cases, the interpretation of generally known facts is my own. In all cases, I have cited my references as I have used them.

Over many decades as I have evolved this work, I have drawn upon old fashioned periodicals and books, to include encyclopedias, as shown below.

Anderson, Walter Truett, "Food Without Farms," (The Biotech Revolution in Agriculture) *Futurist* Jan.-Feb. 1990, pp. 16-21

Berry, Brian, *The Next Ten Thousand Years*, The New American Library, pp. 36-7 (N.S. Kardashev "Statement")

"Common Sense Alternatives," Biomagnetic Catalog, Box 850, Brookline MA 02147

Cornish, Edward, "The Computerized Society," *World Future Society*, Bethesda, Md., 1985

Goldsmith, Joel S., Defense Monitor, *Newsletter*, Vol. XVIII, NO. 4, 1989, p. 1

Hoffman, Kenneth A., "Ancient Magnetic Reversals: Clues to the Geo-dynamo," *Scientific American*, May 1988, p. 76

Hogue, John, *Nostradamus and the Millennium*, Doubleday & Co., NY 1987, p. 172

Insight Magazine, "Cracking Weather Secrets," 1-9-89, p. 81.

Kushi, Michio, "Experience the Miracle of Life," *East-West Health Books*, Brookline, MA, 1985

Lewis, Richard S., *Illustrated Encyclopedia of the Universe*, 1983 Harmony Books, NY, p. 21

Lewis, Richard S., ibid, p. 55

Lovelock, James, *The Ages of Gaia*, W.W. Norton & Co. NY

MacLaine, Shirley, Going Within, (A Guide to Inner Transformation), Bantam Books, NY, 1989

Nakagawa, Dr. Kyoichi, "Magnetic Field Deficiency Syndrome and Magnetic Treatment," *Japanese Journal*, No. 2475, Dec. 4, 1976

Noone, Richard W., 5/5/2000, *ICE: The Ultimate Disaster*, Harmony House, 1986, p. 53

Science Digest, Oct. 1959, p. 65

Spence, Lewis, *The Encyclopedia of the Occult*, Bracken Books,

London, pp. 436-7

Time-Life Books, *Mind Over Matter*, 1988

Trefil, James, "The Cycle of Fate," *Modern Maturity*, Dec. 1989-Jan. 1990 pp. 60-64

White, John, *Pole Shift*, A.R.E. Press, Virginia Beach, VA, 1980,

p. xxiv

World Almanac, 1985, p. 359

World Book Encyclopedia, 1958, Vol. 7, pp. 2924-2925

World Book Encyclopedia, 1985, Vol. A, p. 840

World Watch Magazine, March-April 1989, p. 43

York Dispatch (newspaper), York, PA., Nov. 20, 1989

INDEX